# THE LONGMYND ADVENTURE CAMP, AND ME
# The Final Chapter

Alan Scriven MBE

HEDDON PUBLISHING

First edition published in 2021 by Heddon Publishing.



ISBN 978-1-913166-44-1

Cover design by Catherine Clarke

www.heddonpublishing.com
www.facebook.com/heddonpublishing
@PublishHeddon

I dedicate this book to every soul, living and departed, who between 1958 and 1998 helped in whatever capacity they could to make the Longmynd Adventure Camp the undisputed success that it became.

Also, to you, my readers: thank you for your continued support. I am very grateful to you.

But most especially to all the lads, who like me were very blessed to be given a countryside experience at one of the prettiest locations in this ancient island of ours.

So, there was then after all, something very valuable to be gained from being classed as "socially deprived".

Every cloud...

# Prologue

This is my third book about the Longmynd Adventure Camp, a registered children's charity (no. 508293), which has its roots in the rear garden of a (now) former police house on the A49 at Wistanstow, between Church Stretton and Craven Arms in Shropshire.

Readers of my previous books will know that it all began in the summer of 1958, when a South Shropshire police constable and his wife provided a country break for a handful of young, socially deprived lads from the urban districts of the West Midlands. And "the Camp" is still operating today, albeit in a noticeably different format from the one intended by its founder, Mr W.F. (Bill) Williams BEM. That said, I must concede that Bill, in his final years, came to accept how the Camp's use had changed. That's not to say he entirely agreed with it, but it at least ensured, I suppose, some form of continuity. At the time of Bill's passing, he had been re-connected to his Camp for a number of years, by way of a "life presidency" role, and was also involved again with working on Camp (a day here and a day there) with me... after seven long years of no contact at all!

Before gaining official charity status, the Camp was called the WVS BOYS CAMP. This was in recognition of the Women's Voluntary Service, which originally agreed to select, and indeed sponsor, the boys from Wolverhampton and Birmingham, who would be offered a ten-day basic camping holiday in the heart of the South Shropshire countryside, wherever Bill managed to obtain permission to set up.

Readers of my first two books on the history of this once wonderful and popular place will know that I am myself a former beneficiary of the Camp, who went on to become its overall leader in 1990, after the late great Bill Williams BEM ended his tenure as “Skipper”.

To re-cap: my association with the Camp began in 1965 when, as a twelve-year-old, I was given the opportunity to join my elder brother Billy on a “holiday of a lifetime”. Billy had been very fortunate to be selected for a place at the Camp in 1964, so was able to advise me, and frighten me, with stories of this strange-sounding place.

After a “career” with the Camp lasting thirty-three years (man and boy), during which time I held all positions with the exception of Cook and Bursar/QM, I amassed a great deal of knowledge and memorabilia, which has proved to be of great benefit to me in writing this, and my previous books *The Longmynd Adventure Camp and Me* and *More from The Longmynd Adventure Camp, and Me*, published by Shropshire-based Heddon Publishing, and available in paperback and Kindle form.

Having been asked to write a third book on the same subject, I initially played around with a couple of ideas. In fact, I got some six thousand words into a book featuring a selection of different days at the LAC over its first forty years, which is the time period of its now sixty-two-year history that my previous books cover.

I broke all ties with the Camp in 1998, its fortieth year, due to an obvious policy change. The format in which it had operated was, apparently, no longer acceptable, so I felt I had no option. I could have remained as a member of the committee, but I considered this to be a hypocritical act if I didn't agree with how the Camp was going to continue. And continue it has done... and how! The charity professes still to offer holidays to the kind of child it was originally founded for (this is obviously a condition of its continued charity status, which the original committee fought so hard to achieve), but in my opinion it hasn't done so, at least not in the fashion that it used to, pre-1998. 1997 saw the final Camp in the format we had worked to since its inception, but the following year was to be our Ruby anniversary; that's the saddest thing about it. There was no celebration of a fantastic achievement, and not one single effort by the committee to even recognise it! I considered that sad fact to be unacceptable in the extreme.

The dramatic finale of the ever-growing strangulation - by so called "red tape" - of our way (the tried and tested way) of doing it is explained in detail in my first book. Please don't misunderstand me; I know and appreciate that as time evolved, so the Camp had to. I was prepared for this.

The way in which the changes came, and the speed with which

they occurred, however, were shocking and disappointing to the extreme, given that they entirely changed the way the Camp was run, with little to no regard for its origins. They also put paid to the ruby anniversary celebrations we had planned.

Many years after the event, I have been presented with some interesting correspondence, which might suggest that there was more going on behind the scenes. It is possible that some of the committee members were privy to this, which might go some way to explaining their lack of support for me. I will go into more detail about this in due course.

Regarding this third book, I decided, after much consideration, to go down the path of what I hope will be interesting facts, and some figures, from over the years, as well as one or two stories of my time with the Camp, and my life away from it; before and after, because I considered (based on comments made to me regarding my earlier books) that perhaps this might be of interest to the thousands of people who at some point in their lives were a part of this then wonderful haven, far from the hustle and bustle of everyday life; whether they were a beneficiary, or a voluntary member of staff, for just one year, or many, or perhaps an official of the WRVS (now the RVS), which selected and sponsored the children.

During my long association with this much-needed charity, for which I was awarded the MBE in 2001, I literally kept everything that came into my possession. And when I told our founder and leader Bill Williams BEM that I wanted to write the history of the Camp, he very kindly helped me with a few facts and figures, as well as offering all the paperwork he himself had amassed. I am therefore in a good position to go ahead with this book, which I hope you will enjoy.

I will not be quoting facts and figures of results of cabin/tent competitions, sports day, and personal awards from 1990, as these are already listed in my first book. But I will include, as far as is possible, and certainly from 1990, the names of every child who shared the Camp with us, in the hope that some, if not all of them, will see their name, which I hope will evoke some pleasant memories of their time at the Longmynd Adventure Camp. I will also include the identity of all volunteers from that period, and previous, where my records provide, and at the end of the book (as with my previous books) I will list yet more people who in their own way gave whatever they could to assist the growth and continuation of a dream which so many shared, and coaxed into reality.

Towards the end of this book, the reader will be treated to a very beautiful poem, the work of a very dear friend, Owen J. Lewis of Shrewsbury. Owen is a former tent leader, who was invited to help at Camp by Bill (as told in my first book - page 214). He is a writer, poet, and playwright (Google him) and I am honoured that he has agreed to contribute to my books.

Owen's poem is a very pleasant and poignant look-back to

what Camp meant: who it was for, and what it was all about. He tells a story which not only offers a fitting end to my trilogy of books about a truly unforgettable little spot in the very heart of South Shropshire, but also of the one man who, with an ongoing group of volunteers, made it all possible. The poem is set in Minton Batch.

I will include some facts and stories about that area, which was loved by the children and staff who came to the Camp from far and wide. It is a valley which was heavily involved in every year of the Camp as we knew it!

Also, the beautiful little town of Church Stretton played a considerable part every year: shopping for presents, swimming in the school pool, playing football and other games in the park, as well as practising for Campfire skits and the like. Occasional trips to see the local GP (Doctor Gooch when I was a boy), or the dentist. Making use of the local hostelries from time to time. It all happened in Church Stretton, so I'll do it justice, I hope, by mentioning a few facts about its very interesting history.

If you chance upon the Longmynd Adventure Camp, which is now a first-rate facility, used largely for schools, Scout Groups, D of E Award base, etc., please spare a thought for its founder, the late great Bill Williams BEM, and the rear garden of a police house in Wistanstow, where it all began, back in 1958.

# Chapter One

My second book began with a few words from Bill Williams. I thought it might benefit readers to know a little about his early life. And I consider now that Bill's time as the "village bobby" in Wistanstow, where he himself said he had the best years of his police career, would be worth including. Therefore, my first chapter is dedicated to my late great mentor and friend, Mr Bill Williams BEM; in his own words.

*I was posted to Wistanstow (near Craven Arms) from Bridgnorth, as a rural Beat Officer in 1954; so began a very interesting and a very different lifestyle. The police house was on the main A49 Hereford to Shrewsbury road, at Grove Bank. As this was before the opening of the M6 motorway, the road carried a tremendous amount of traffic, including heavy goods vehicles, from South Wales to the north of England; the road was very busy, continuously, night and day.*

*The police house was a semi-detached with a large garden, at the bottom of which was a busy railway line, and also a railway halt, which Dr Beeching closed when he "modernised" the railway system.*

*Our water supply came from a well in a yard at the back of the house. The water had to be pumped up to a storage tank in the house by a hand-operated pump in the kitchen. Hetty, my wife, always said that, thanks to this regular exercise, she had one breast more developed than the other! Eventually, we had an electric pump installed.*

*There was an old-fashioned telephone under the stairs on the ground floor; no extension for night calls, but eventually we did get an office (of sorts) in the side garden. A friendly Post Office engineer, no BT in those days, came and supplied and fitted an extension in the house, under the stairs... no charge.*

*Sometime later, the Police Authority decided to provide a wooden building in the side garden, and this became my police office.*

*Due to my ongoing involvement with the Rowing Club, and other things, I returned to Bridgnorth in my spare time. Life in Wistanstow, however, was to become a totally new experience for me; becoming part of a community, for instance. The village school; the village pub; the church; the district nurse (who lived in a cottage attached to the village hall); the shop, and me, the village constable, made everyone who lived in the village a real community. I refer to Wistanstow because that's where I lived, but it was the same for people in the many other villages. And I always realised and accepted that my responsibilities and influence extended throughout the whole of my "beat".*

*How times have changed! One received so much respect and support from the whole community. You felt part of it; not isolated or feared, but respected... or at least what you stood for was respected. As an individual, respect had to be earned. And, as a village policeman, to a great degree I was left to make my own decisions on how I dealt with different situations, and you could do this, with a well-founded knowledge of the characters and personalities of the people you were dealing with.*

*One of the problems I encountered as the village bobby was the gypsy fraternity. Some of them were genuine Romanies, and reasonably easy to deal with, and many of them, of course, I got to know quite well by meeting them a number of times during the year. Most of them travelled by horse-drawn caravans, not all in motor vehicles as they do today. I remember one occasion when I was called to the small village of Affcot, where I found about six caravans, plus lorries (and ponies) parked up near the side of the River Onny, near Craven Arms. There were about ten men, every one of them at least six feet tall; big and brawny, with red hair, all of them, together with their women and children. And as the river was well stocked with trout by the estate, and local landowners, the gypsies were not welcomed with open arms! It was extremely difficult to move them on; not an easy task - cunning and diplomacy needing to be employed. There were offences committed, i.e. camping on the highway; lighting fires on the highway, etc, worthless to pursue, as by the time any action was decided, they would be long gone. I did manage to move them on, but when I returned to ensure they had departed, lined up along the riverbank, presumably for my benefit, were the remains of a large number of trout skeletons.*

*My area of responsibility stretched from the boundary of Craven Arms to the boundary of Church Stretton, which had its own police sergeant and two constables, as did Craven Arms. It was the sergeant at Church Stretton who I was responsible to; I took in all the villages between the towns, including Little Stretton, Affcot, Bushmoor, Cheyney Longville, and many others. But the most important of my duties was the main A49. Fatal accidents were common on this very busy road, and whenever one happened, you were on your own! There was a transport cafe between the two towns (still there today) called the Lazy Trout, and this was a popular refreshment stop for the many long-distance lorry drivers. It wasn't unusual to see anything up to about fifty lorries parked up at the café, or even on the road nearby. Very often, owners of the various companies for whom the drivers worked would show up to pay them off; and numerous "ladies of the night" would be in the café, plying their "trade". It did become somewhat of a black spot for accidents at one stage.*

*To patrol the beat, I used a 150cc BSA Bantam motorcycle, then later a 250cc Ariel Leader, which was equipped with a radio, which meant that, for the first time, I was in contact with Headquarters.*

*There was a super village school in Wistanstow, which my*

*elder daughter Ann attended from the age of five; with Debbie following in due course.*

*At the age of eleven, Ann attended St Winifred's Convent School in Shrewsbury, travelling each day on the bus. How we managed to achieve this, I cannot now imagine. Although I don't remember the cost of her fares, they were not enormous, but on my salary of five guineas per week (which was actually quite a good income for those times), it was difficult some weeks. In addition to my salary, however, we had no rent or rates to pay on the police house.*

*Soon after being posted to Wistanstow, I decided to start a youth club in the village hall; a superb mock-Tudor building that included a cottage for the use of the District Nurse, and another for the resident caretaker.*

*This fantastic facility had been provided for the village by the family that owned The Grove; an enormous and beautiful house in very extensive grounds, through which the River Onny flowed, and complete with stabling and numerous cottages.*

*There were great things to come from this youth club; all the activities we did were simply suggested, discussed, and then implemented by the committee. I have so many memories of this great club, some of which I feel are well worth recording:*

*The Village Hall had a good stage, and we entered many events, including the County Youth Drama Festival, which was organised by the County Youth Service. This organisation was of great help; we began to do concerts at Christmas, which we rehearsed before performing them at the care homes for the elderly, and it was so amazing to witness the pleasure gained by elderly and young alike. Such happy memories from Ludlow, Church Stretton, Bishop's Castle, and other places.*

*I also had the enjoyment of my daughter Ann performing with me at these simple little concerts; we did the song 'Mother dear come bathe my forehead', together, and more of the old songs, which were enjoyed by all ages. We also entered the County Youth Drama Festival; we didn't win, but we did get to the finals.*

*Christmas was always a busy time. Carol singing for a charity was a must, and we didn't only sing on doorsteps, we went to all the care homes, and we also sang in all the village pubs for miles around. One of the older people in the village, Tom Cadwallader, would accompany us on his old slide trombone. All very simple, full of joy, and a lot of money raised for various charities.*

*It was about this time, whilst the club was a member of the Shropshire Association of Youth Clubs, that I became voluntary Field Officer for the Association, and spent even more time visiting other voluntary clubs throughout the county, helping with planning and introducing activities, which included (believe it or not) piano-smashing competitions, as well as many other activities including sponsored walks and the like.*

*We did a great deal for our community, and for the Church. Our village church, when I arrived in Wistanstow, had an elderly clergyman, who wasn't the slightest bit interested in the club or anything else, outside of the Church. As an example, one of the activities was the Harvest Festival; no great deal but we decided we would like to have a festival in some local pubs including The Plough at Wistanstow, and The Green Dragon in Little Stretton. Not only to celebrate harvest, but also to raise money for charity by the sale of the produce that people had donated. I visited the rector and asked if he would take a service in The Plough. He declined, saying he didn't approve... but we went ahead and did it anyway. I found a young priest from, I think, a village near Clun, who defied the rector, and took the service in the pub. It was a huge success, and we did it annually for a number of years after, in many other pubs, too.*

*When the rector retired, a new vicarage was built. This brought Archdeacon John Lewis, a married man with a delightful family, to the village. This family made a huge difference to village life, thus strengthening the Church by their keen enthusiasm. Richard*, John's son (now retired Bishop of Edmundsbury and Ipswich), became a very active member of the youth club, as did his younger sister, Mags. I served on the altar, as did other members, and this brought the church and the club closer together.*

*Debbie's christening was really a joint effort between ourselves and both the Anglican and Catholic clergy. The nearest Roman Catholic Church was in the tiny village of*

*Plowden, between Craven Arms and Bishop's Castle. Our Catholic priest, Father Louis Catteral, was everything you would expect of a Christian; looking after his flock, travelling round his parishes on a AJS motorcycle (no such luxury as a car). He was to be minister of the service, but we had to get there in the snow, and we hadn't a car, either. No problem. Our new C of E parish rector, Archdeacon Lewis, drove us to the little Catholic church, and even attended the service. This was ecumenism at its best.*

*Christmas times became very busy. We had our party in the village hall, and we started a senior citizens club. The Christmas party still happens today, which is testament to the commitment of all involved. And carol singing, which raised more money for charity, was another activity of the stalwarts, among whom were Roy Williams**, a resident of the village and a very dear friend. Roy had a very good bass voice and was very musical.*

*On Christmas mornings, we visited a number of elderly people who lived alone, taking presents purchased from funds raised by other activities we did. We also delivered Christmas dinner to a number of those who did not have anyone to visit them.*

*I remember going to an elderly gentleman who lived alone, to take his Christmas dinner. As expected, he wasn't at home. I guessed correctly that he was in the pub. He was a grumpy old soul, but he and I got along fine. He said, 'Take it back to my house and put it in the oven.' I said no, because we had other deliveries to make. I served it up to him there and then.*

*The meals were prepared and donated by two men who owned and ran a restaurant in Church Stretton, and the meals were top quality. They even organised transport, and accompanied us on our deliveries. People were so kind and helpful back then.*

*I was still the village policeman, however, but in the main, able to work hours to suit myself, and the job.*

*It was not unusual to receive anonymous telephone calls from people out to cause trouble for their enemies, or to try and get revenge. One that comes to mind was a report that a drunk was in the village pub, and he had a motorcycle on the car park. I visited the pub and had a word with the landlord, an ex-AA patrol man. The motorcyclist was drunk, so we took the valves out of bike tyres and put them behind the bar for him to collect the next day. Common sense and "summary justice" were exercised, rather than the letter of the law.*

*Some rather unpleasant memories include the task of having to remove from the railway tracks the body of a woman who had committed suicide by jumping in front of the train. This was a bucket and shovel job, with no other public service involved except the policeman and the undertaker!*

*Another suicide I was called to attend in the early hours involved an old man who had been suffering from cancer. He lived with his family in an isolated cottage a few miles from Wistanstow. I arrived to find the poor man sitting in the outside privy down the garden, with a 12-bore shotgun between his knees, and what was left of his head all over the wall of the privy. I reported it to my local sergeant, who attended. It proved a most difficult and formidable task, getting the body out of the privy and down the garden path to the waiting hearse.*

*That said, and despite other unpleasant situations, I do believe my days in Wistanstow were among the best of my life.*

*The Diseases of Animals Acts were, in those far-off days, administered by the Police. As the village bobby, I issued all the movement certificates required to move animals from one farm to another. I also supervised the sheep dipping, issuing the necessary paperwork for this. I had to ensure (by visiting all the farms) that the sheep were dipped at the appropriate time; even the sheep on the Long Mynd hills. The local hill farmers would provide me with a pony to accompany them, and ensure clearance and dipping. What fun this was... and the tricks that were played. What pony I got depended on the farmer. It could be one in foal, which meant that when riding downhill, you slid onto its neck. Or it might be extremely fast... or slow, or it could hardly run at all. I was not the best horseman, but it was a great few days out. Pole Cottage, at the top of the hill, was the place where we gathered at the end of the clearance. It was like a scene from the Wild West, with beer in quantity, and ponies and farmers all around.*

So then... a policeman's lot could be a happy one!

*Richard Lewis (now retired Bishop) was to become a member of Bill's voluntary staff at Camp in the mid-sixties. We chose Richard to "officiate" at the unveiling ceremony of Bill's memorial bench (more details further into this book).

**Roy Williams was also destined to join Bill's voluntary staff, almost from the outset.

# Chapter Two

The child beneficiaries of the Longmynd Adventure Camp were considered socially deprived, and by some to be unloved by their families, which was patently untrue. The truth was, however, we did not have a lot, and our families often endured hardship. My own mother suffered the pain of experiencing two stillbirths, and raised five children single-handed, with very few resources. For us children, it was a case of having to push ourselves if we wished to achieve in life. It would be harder than for those who had wealthy, or even comfortably-off, families, but there is a saying, *Where there's a will there's a way*, and I like to think I am living proof of the truth in this.

At primary school (Woden Road, Heath Town, Wolverhampton) we had regular handwriting tests before we were judged to be good enough to be given a pen nib and ink well. I was the first child in my year to achieve this "honour".

I was the only one of my mother's offspring to go out and get a newspaper delivery job to help with the extremely tight family budget; in fact, I got myself a position at two newsagents in Low Hill.

I became involved in amateur dramatics at senior school (Springfield Secondary Modern), and I got into the football team, and the choir. I was regularly chosen to read the lesson at morning assembly. My best friend all through school and to this day, Kenny Turner, and I were the dinner monitors for the teachers for almost three of the four years we spent at that great school. I tell a couple of light-hearted stories about Kenny and me in my previous books.

In my working career, which is still ongoing as I write (I left school at fifteen years of age in 1968 with not one qualification), I managed at almost every company I have worked for, to reach the top. I hold a Class 1 PCV licence, and I am a qualified JCB (3C) Operator.

I am very different from my siblings, and to my mind, that's not a bad thing. I have never really enjoyed a good relationship with any of them; not lasting, anyway. My late siblings Pat (1947-2003) and Billy (1952-2016) were perhaps the best of the bunch as we were growing up. I enjoyed a good brotherly relationship with David, who joined me at Camp as a member of staff... and an excellent one, without doubt. Sadly, as with many families, we have had our share of disagreements and at the time of writing, David and I are not in touch with one another, but I have always made sure he is invited and welcome to attend all events relating to the Longmynd Adventure Camp.

After leaving school, I was invited for trials with Coventry City and Walsall Football Clubs. But, like so many young hopefuls who thought they had stardust in their boots, mine were judged to be full of sand.

However, I was a very good footballer, and played regularly on Saturdays and Sundays in the Wolverhampton works, and amateur leagues. It was during this time in my life that I was asked to manage a local boys' football team. I agreed with a neighbour, Mr Bevan, to give it one season. We won two trophies!

I learnt my football skills playing in the street with my brothers and friends. If I'm honest, our Billy was the best of the three of us, but he was never interested enough to try and take it any further. He was happy just to play wherever we decided, as a group, to play. We had lots of choices besides the street. The old field between Fifth Avenue and Fourth Avenue was a regular venue; not ideal, but local to us all. Our footballing friends included Tony and Colin Brewer (Tony the stand-out player of us all. He was just as good in goal as outfield; a really great player), and Anthony Sweet, who lived towards the bottom end of Fifth Avenue. Sometimes, especially on dry summer evenings and occasional weekends, we would all troop off to Showell Circus, and join up with our friends from different streets to play on one of the quarters of the circular park; we played on all four over the years. Actually, ball games were prohibited, so as we played, we would have one eye on the gates as we looked out for the grumpy old park-keeper.

We also made good and regular use of Fowler's Park, and the Wolverhampton Transport Club. Football was our life, growing up. If we weren't playing it, we would be watching Wolves at

Molineux, if our meagre finances allowed.

We never got pocket money in our house, and we never had the luxury of taking mid-morning lunch to school. Breakfast consisted (almost every school morning) of a couple of slices of toast and five malted milk biscuits. On some cold winter mornings, Mom would give us a bowl of porridge oats.

I am the only member of my maternal family, for as far back as I have researched (sixteenth century), to be awarded royal recognition for voluntary charity work.

I have also appeared on television programmes such as The Money Programme with the news presenter Sophie Raworth (we even shared a taxi from the Custard Factory to Birmingham Railway Station after recording it); and one episode of the Australian soap, *Home and Away*. This came about after the production team contacted us at Wellington Bus Depot. They were interested in borrowing a bus (and driver) for a scene in Ironbridge. Peter Ralphs, the depot manager, agreed, and suggested that I asked to be in a scene. Amazingly, they agreed, so I asked my colleague Ian Tully to drive the bus. He agreed, and I boarded it as one or two of the regular cast boarded or alighted. Great fun!

In the 1980s, I was chosen as a so-called "Page 7 fella", after being spotted in Wolverhampton's Mander Centre by a representative of the *Sun* newspaper.

I met the late actor Pete Postlethwaite a number of times,

actor Dennis Waterman, and the incomparable George Best. Recently, I was delighted to meet former SAS Sergeant Major Mark "Billy" Billingham, of Channel 4 series *SAS Who Dares Wins*. We had a chat after his show at Stafford Gatehouse Theatre. I am also good friends with Joanna Roundell-Greene, a granddaughter of the former Prime Minister, Clement Atlee. Jo is featured in my first book. She kindly volunteered her help on Camp in 1981 and 1982.

So, all in all, not bad, you might think, for a snotty-nosed scruff from a largely poor council estate in north Wolverhampton.

To me, however, my biggest achievement was my success with the Longmynd Adventure Camp. From a twelve-year-old boy who had hardly let go of his mother's apron strings, and who had very limited travelling experiences, or life experiences – save living in the continual struggle of having no excesses but poverty – I made my steady way through "the ranks" to become a proud second-in-command to the one man whom I held the highest respect for... totally and completely... even during the lost years, and every sad episode in our friendship which they brought: so much sadness that every one of my terms as his replacement was scarred with losing that friendship for almost seven years. Thoughts of betrayal, guilt and regret have never left me. Even considering the fact that at that awful meeting in 1989 (as described in my first book), I made what I honestly believed to be the right decision at that moment in time. But, as I've said previously, we all have degrees in hindsight!

I discovered, quite by chance, and to my absolute amazement, that my biological father (whom sadly I never knew) was an American soldier! It was kept from me from the outset, by my mother and everyone else who knew. I have my own ideas as to why she kept it a secret from me; but I had a right to know. And I am not the slightest bit interested in other people's opinions on why she thought it best that I wasn't told. I knew I was different from my siblings; people used to comment on this throughout my childhood. I repeatedly asked my mother about my real father's identity, but received the same response every time: 'Don't be silly, Alan. Stop asking stupid questions.'

This is what I know now from eventual conversations (no one wanted to talk about it, because my mother had sworn them all to secrecy) with other family members who knew before I did: my father was an American soldier, with the rank of Sergeant, who met my mother through another family member, who offered to help him find (or at least some details about) his British roots. They "hit it off" whilst my mother lived in her parents' house in Fifth Avenue (where I lived all my life until I married Tina). He wanted my mother (with Pat and Billy) to go to the US when he was told that she was pregnant with me. My dad wanted me to be born in America, and to raise a family which would include Pat and Billy, but Mother refused. I am told that her reason(s) for refusing included the deteriorating health of her mother... and the fact that my grandmother was dead-set against the idea anyway: 'You're not running off with these kids for some Yank!' was the put-down she used, apparently.

Whatever the truth of this whole sad affair, my father flew back to the States (because he had no option), but returned again some years later, as a civilian, to try again; even asking, apparently, if he could take me back, if not her and the now extended family. And again, his kind suggestion fell on deaf ears! I use the term "kind" because he obviously loved me, and I am certain in my mind that he would have been a good dad; maybe that's where I get it from... I hope so.

How I wish my dear aunt Emma had lived long enough to tell me about my father. She would have done, I know she would. Aunt Emma (as I mention in my previous books) died very early, at the young age of just thirty-nine years old. I loved her; she was a truly lovely lady, but that said, you crossed her at your peril! She, like her sister (my mother) called a spade a spade. Uncle Harold found himself on the receiving end of Emma's always justifiable rants more than a time or two!

It is sad to think that I knew Emma better than the youngest of her children did. My cousin Christine was barely at school at the time of her mother's untimely passing, so has little memory of her. And it's the same for her siblings, Peter, and Edward, who was just a baby. But they can take pride in the fact that their mother loved all her children dearly.

Part of my early childhood involved spending time in a children's home in Wednesfield, Wolverhampton. The Cottage Homes was the scourge of children like me back in the day. My two brothers, Billy and David (b.1954), and my sister Pat, were put into the home for a period of time, in order to give our mother some respite from the hardship of raising children in the 1950s with nothing but a meagre National Assistance weekly handout. It carried on well into the sixties, too; watching every penny! Mealtimes are most memorable: we would all squash in front of the oven to try and get warm for a few minutes before it was turned off!

I've already mentioned our breakfasts, but our evening meal was usually (in winter) breast of lamb, or rabbit stew. The rabbits were a gift from one of Mom's friends, and breast of lamb was dirt-cheap back then. But you ate what was put in front of you; no menu!! My eldest sister Pat turned her nose up at a bowl of stew one evening, so Mom took it away, saying there was nothing else. 'Fine,' said Pat, 'I'll do without.'

The next morning, our mother put yesterday's stew in front of Pat. 'There's your breakfast.'

'I'm not eating that, Mom. I told you last night.'

'An' I told you, there's nothing else. I can't afford to waste food. So you'll get nothing else until you eat this stew.'

It became a stand-off, but there was only ever going to be one winner. On the third day, Pat reluctantly ate the stew. You could keep stew a few days without it losing any of its goodness and flavours... even without a fridge!

We never had a fridge. Mother would use the cold slab in the pantry for saucepans of food, because the lids would keep the mice out!!

I mean no disrespect to my late mother, who loved and looked after all of us with a commitment second to none. But I had a right to know the truth about my father. I should have been told about his identity (I asked her often enough) whilst there was still a chance of at least trying, even after all the intervening years, to make contact with him.

But now that will never happen!

I am proud of my mother for the way she stuck to her commitments regarding raising us with so very little. I am also proud of my own achievements. And I am proud of my dad. From everything I have been told about him, he was a good man, who wanted to accept me, and the responsibilities of fatherhood, given the chance. And he was a good soldier, who served his country – my Fatherland – to the best of his ability. God bless you, sir.

Strangely, when I was a young lad, between the age of about seven and ten years old, I had occasional "episodes" of acting as an American soldier! I know it's easy for me to say this now, but it is the truth. Secondly, anyone who really knows me (I'm not the easiest person in the world to know; I have a very small number of trusted friends, and I can be more than a little rude and dismissive, not to mention anti-social, and a tad sarcastic when the mood takes me) will know that I have always had a "pull" towards America. Got to mean something, surely?

And yes, I have visited the United States.

# Chapter Three

After a very successful “dry run”, Shropshire police constable Bill Williams made what turned out to be a monumental decision.

In the summer of 1958, he and his lovely wife Hetty, in conjunction with the Women’s Voluntary Service, took a handful of young lads from the poorer districts of the West Midlands, and gave them a Camping experience in the rear garden of his police house on the A49 at Wistanstow, near Craven Arms. It was a huge success, so much so that Bill made that monumental decision: to do it again the following year, with many more children – twenty-seven, in fact – on any piece of land that was offered to him by a Hamperley farmer whom he considered a friend. Bill explained what he wanted, and needed, to Brian Jones, who kindly gave Bill his blessing to use one of his fields at Minton Oaks; thereby giving rise to the “WVS Boys Camp”. Not many people know, however, that his “project” was almost called “Shropshire Boys Camp”. Perhaps it was the fact that none of the boys hailed from Shropshire (until years later) that changed all that.

The 1960 Camp was held in the same field; Brian proved to be the friend Bill knew him to be. The fact that he was the local bobby never came into Brian’s mind!

Bill's Camp was another success, which only added to his dream of making the experience that approximately sixty or so young socially deprived lads had already enjoyed a permanent fixture in future years. It now seemed overwhelmingly likely that Brian's field in Hamperley was to be the setting for a grounding of sorts for Bill's future Camps. Alas, however, it wasn't to be, and through no fault of the kind farmer.

The Camp of 1961 was situated in a field at the top of Long Lane in Craven Arms. A derelict building called Endeavour Cottage stood next to the field at Hammonds Green, and whoever owned it (I have no details of who this was) gave permission for it to be used, as well as the field. So, the lads camped in tents, and on occasions took their meals inside the old cottage, which was also used for some indoor games when the weather wasn't agreeable.

Strangely then, one might think, Bill again sought the help of Mr Jones the farmer, for Camp no. 4 (excluding the original police house garden venture). And even stranger when you consider that it wasn't the field that had held successful Camps in 1959 and 1960; no, it was the field at the entrance of Minton Batch (to the left as one enters the valley). Perhaps permission for the cottage was granted for one Camp only?

During one of many chats with Bill with regards to my writing a book on the history of the Camp (how I wish I had committed myself to doing it sooner, before he passed away), the question of why he left Brian after two successful years, and then returned two years later, did come up. Bill, however, couldn't remember, so I left it at that. I'm happy to say now, though, that the mystery was solved just after the publication of my first book.

I wasn't sure whether or not Brian Jones was still with us because he must have been "getting on" in 2017. Moreover, was he still living at the farm? I decided to try and find out.

Armed with a signed copy of my book, complete with a personal message to Brian, I drove to Hamperley Farm. The reason for my visit was nothing to do with the question I had put to Bill; I wanted to give Brian a copy of the book, by way of a thank you for his kindness all those years ago. I parked just inside the entrance and closed the gate. Immediately, an intensely evocative feeling overcame me as I slowly, very slowly, walked up the driveway. I was filled with wonderment about the Camps that had taken place at this very spot almost sixty years ago! I knew exactly where the Camp had been set up, from my vast collection of photographs, and others that have been kindly given by Bill's daughters, Ann and Debbie.

I saw through my mind's eye the "pioneers" who had laid the foundations of today's Longmynd Adventure Camp, situated (since 1980) just a few hundred yards away. No one, I considered, connected with the charity today (with possibly the exception of one person) could even begin to imagine where its roots took hold, or even how it got to what it was when we all regrettably had to say goodbye in the late nineties... unless they have read my books?

I eventually reached the gate of the farmhouse (it's a fair stroll, even when one is not thinking deeply about the history of one of its fields) and my nerves were doing their best to get the better of me. I stood, wondering if this was a good idea, or should I turn now, before anyone would have any clue that I had been. Then I heard the front door open, and as I looked down the path, a frail and elderly gentleman appeared.

'Hello! Who are you? What do you want?'

Mr Jones had lost his wife a few years earlier. She would have recognised me, I think! Mary (Preece as was) would regularly come and say hello to us when we were at Camp. My friend John Preece (the cook at Camp for fifteen years) got talking with her about possible family connections a time or two; and he said they had found one, too.

I hadn't seen Brian for a long time, though, so had to introduce myself:

'Morning Brian, I'm Alan Scriven from the Longmynd Adventure Camp; a friend of Bill's. Bill Williams,' I called to him as he stood stock-still by the door.

'Oh hi, how is he?'

I had to tell Brian that Bill had unfortunately passed away in 2013. He was quite shocked. He began walking slowly towards me.

'Bloody hell, Alan, I thought I'd have gone before Bill. That's a bugger, poor bloke.'

'Yes, Brian. It was quite sudden; he'd had a fall,' I explained.

'Bloody good bloke, was Bill; good copper as well.'

'He was, Brian, I thought the world of him; he was like a dad in my eyes.'

'Well, you would'na done better than ol' Bill, that's for sure.' By this time, he was just casually holding onto the gate for a bit of support. 'What can I do for you then, Alan?'

I explained that I had written a book on the history of the Camp, and that I had brought him a copy as a small token of thanks for all he had done for Bill and his boys during the Camp's infancy; and later in 1981. He was delighted that I had remembered him. And without further ado, he launched straight into telling me that he'd wanted Bill to remain on his farm, with the Camp. But at the end of the 1960 Camp, Bill told Brian, apparently, that he would look elsewhere for a place for the following year. He told me that Bill had said he was grateful but didn't want to push it.

And then... Brian told me that the real reason was (apparently, he emphasised) because the neighbours were against having the "type of child" the WVS Boys Camp catered for. And also, he added, because they were "very noisy".

'I never heard much of the kids, though, and neither did the missus. He should have stuck with it; this place, I mean, because no one ever came complaining at my door, an' in any case, I'd have given 'em their answer if they had.' He chuckled a little, and I joined in.

I decided to let Mr Jones get on with his day. But just before I did, I had an idea. 'By the way Brian,' I began nervously. 'I do a bit of metal detecting, and I wondered whether you'd mind me doing a bit on the field where the Camps were held.' White lie coming up: 'Only, I remember Bill saying he'd lost a ring on your field, which was never found. I just might find it for his family; what do you think?'

'Yes, no problem, just come when you're ready.'

We shook hands, he thanked me again for the book, then admitted he'd probably never read it (bless him), and I walked away, after making sure he got back to his front door okay.

The white lie had just come out. I had the idea that there would be things worth finding from the two Camps on the field. But to this day, I haven't been back! I have wanted to, but my little misdemeanour still gets the better of my conscience.

There are no surviving records of the Camps prior to 1962, sadly, but Bill's 6d copy of a Red Lion Brand notebook offers quite a few facts regarding 1962, and one or two subsequent Camps:

**Income**

Cheque from WVS: £125 0s 0d

Cash from Mr Williams re: excess food: £1 0s 0d

Donation from Red Lion: £1.4s 6d

Donation from Dennis O'Connor: £0.10s 0d

Donation from James (Jim) Culham: £5 0s 0d

Total Income 1962 Camp: £132 14s 06d

I have all the figures for the 1962 expenditure, too, but perhaps too many items to list here. The actual total cost of this Camp, however, was £135 4s 11d.

Just to mention a few things/provisions purchased:

Paraffin lamps; 56lbs porridge (loose); 4lbs cocoa; 2doz bottles of squash; 7lbs strawberry jam; 7lbs plum jam; 112lbs sugar (what!!!); 25lbs bacon; 16doz eggs.

Then there were the incidentals, i.e. first-aid equipment; torch batteries; travel sickness pills; sports prizes, etc. Oh... and Jack Birch's travel fare.

Jack Birch was another very good friend, who gave Bill a lot of help at the beginning of his project.

So there was no fall-out between Bill and Brian. Bill just considered that it might be best for Brian (because of the apparent attitude of his neighbours) if he found somewhere else to hold his Camp in 1961.

And proof of the above, if it were ever needed, is the fact that Bill asked Brian if he could use another of his fields for the 1962 Camp. Not only did Brian readily agree, but he did the exact same again, nineteen years later.

To close on 1962 with a fact or two, courtesy of letters from the boys to Skipper: Trevor Halloran won the prize for Best Cook (this was Skipper's prize for the lad who had been most helpful to the cook). His prize was an Observer Book - I won a couple of these fine and popular little books - but Trevor doesn't say what the subject of his copy was. Mine, for Best Camper in 1967 was about horses, and I still have it! My only regret about winning the book was that when it was presented to me by the Skipper at the close of the "awards ceremony" at the end of Campfire, I thanked him, and walked back to where I had been sitting with my brothers, and our tent group, intending to ask "Skip" to sign and date it for me... he always signed every book prize he presented. I took it to him when the soup was being served to the guests, but he was busy chatting to some of them. He said he would sign it later for me, but he forgot to. Over the ensuing years, I mentioned it to Bill several times, and he always responded in the same way: 'Bring it back next year and I'll sign it for you.' But I forgot; and the fact that I had even got the book faded from memory as I took on my responsibilities as a member of staff in the ensuing years. Amazing, really, that I still have it, when I consider all the different places I have lived since 1967; carrying it with me (not literally) to every new abode.

Other small possessions I still have from my childhood include a tiny freestanding bookstand, which I made in woodwork lessons during my first year at senior school, a bag of marbles, and a photograph of myself and everyone else at Woden Road School, taken when I was just seven years old.

The weather during the 1962 Camp was "bad", according to Kelvin Joyce (Tent Four) of Bordsley, Birmingham, 12.

Trevor Halloran was also a member of the 1962 Camp, as was Geoffrey Wain, who hailed from Great Barr, Birmingham. Sadly, some of the lads didn't include their names in the letters they wrote to Skipper. He was, however, able to reply if they left their address, by referring to the so-called "case histories" that were supplied by the WVS (as it was then).

A "Master Peter Nicholls" wrote to Bill from his Edgbaston home, promising "to do better next year". I'm guessing he was perhaps talking about his Sports Day performance, or maybe the tent marks competition.

# Chapter Four

One could, I suppose, ponder forever as to the reasons why the Camp "flirted" with different locations during its early years. But the fact is, it did... until settling in Minton during the early sixties.

Again, though, why did Bill leave Brian for the second time, following the success of 1962? That will now remain a secret forever as I didn't put the question to Brian, and I fear it is now too late to do so. There must have been a reason, however, because the field which accommodated Camp '63 wasn't, on the surface anyway, a patch on the ones belonging to Brian Jones. Perhaps Bill had an idea...

Jack Williams of Minton Hamlet, and his family, had farmed cattle and sheep in the area for generations. He lived at the farmhouse with his daughter, and son-in-law Ted Challinor, along with their daughter Carol.

Jack very kindly allowed Bill to set up Camp 1963 in one of his fields opposite Minton Batch. It wasn't the best part of the field, but it was sufficient, if not ideal, and "beggars" can't be "choosers". Bill was given the western edge of the field, but the following year would bring another short move to the top of this very field; and here Bill's Camp would settle for its longest period, until the move to its very own field just up the lane!

At this point, I have to inform the reader that 1963 saw two actual sites used!

My first book tells the reader (on page 14) that Bill set up Camp at Picklescott (by virtue of permission from a Mr Ross Smetcott). But, as I mention above - and Bill confirmed this - Jack's field (between the lane and the brook) was definitely used in the same year. And the reason why Picklescott was used was, I have since discovered, because it had a cottage, and Bill used it for storage, etc; the actual Camp, though, was in Minton. Sadly, however, hardly any records survive from the 1963 Camp, apart from a note Bill made concerning three kind donations:

Gordon Tyldesley gave £2 2s 0d; Gordon Swan donated £1 10s 0d, and Mr and Mrs Alderson of Bridgnorth kindly added £2 0s 0d to the coffers.

One "record" that has gone unnoticed, however, was the number of letters one Trevor Davis of Ladywood, Birmingham, 16, wrote to the Skipper during his years as a beneficiary of Bill's holiday Camps. So I would like to belatedly award Trevor "Most Proficient Letter Writer". Bill always replied to him, as he did to all of us (in time) who, over the years, put pen to paper after our holiday at Camp, and throughout the year. Trevor was also a main contributor to the *Camp Magazine* (mentioned in my previous books).

1962 was the last time that Trevor would have been permitted to have a holiday at Camp, due to his age, so he volunteered himself as a helper.

On 15th July 1963, Trevor told Skipper that he had now left school and started working. His annual holidays, he said, could be taken at any time, so he could come along to Camp to help if Skipper needed him. He also told Bill that his brother John would be coming with him:

*We will come on Saturday afternoon and return home next Sunday afternoon so that our programme at work will not be interrupted.*

I am making the assumption that they were twins, as they were both now working, and had been at Camp together.

*Please write back and tell me all the details. We will both be very happy to see you again.*

Bill did allow Trevor and John to be at Camp because on 7th August 1963, Trevor wrote to thank Bill for "catering for us". He added (bless him): *I trust that you went away feeling the better for us having been there.*

He also said: *About six were crying on the bus because they had to go home, including Fred Bradley.*

Trevor closes by thanking Skipper for another wonderful time, and for the help and assistance received.

Another very regular letter writer was Francis Maguire; his brother Patrick wasn't far behind him on that score, either!

During the 1963 Camp, which enjoyed good weather from day one, Bill had a chat with Jack and Ted about the possibility of holding the 1964 Camp on the other side of the brook, at the top of the field. It would be ideal, Bill explained, because the top half of the field on the eastern side of the brook (still with me?) was relatively flat. Also, it was big enough to house six tents (if six were needed), as well as the marquee, a storage tent, and some makeshift toilets; plus, there was room for a campfire!

To his relief, both men accepted Bill's request; even granting him permission there and then to use the field for all future Camps up to and including 1977. Bill was delighted because, at least for now, he no longer had the worry of finding somewhere each year to set up his Camps for Socially Deprived Children (or "under privileged", as the term was back then).

By way of his massive appreciation and gratitude, and as a thank you, Bill offered to pay a sum each year as a rental agreement of sorts. Initially, Jack and Ted shied away from Bill's well-meant offer, maybe thinking that it might be termed a legal deal. But Bill was a police officer who trusted the farmers, so wanted nothing in writing; he simply insisted on giving something back for their magnanimous generosity.

And so it was set in turf: Bill would use Jack's field, all of it, and even the one behind it, for Games and Sports Day; plus the one which gave access to "our field" (on which we played games like British Bulldog, Farmer and Poacher, etc.) for a peppercorn "rent" of five shillings per year!

The field was used right up to 1977, inclusive; and this amount was never increased! Obviously, as the deadline for the agreed period of use regarding the field approached, Bill began to look elsewhere, to ensure uninterrupted continuity; without any luck, initially.

In fact, he was forced to ask Mr Challinor (who was by this time running the farm's affairs) to extend the time limit. Ted very kindly agreed, so the Camp was safe for another couple of years.

Just before we commit 1963 to the Camp's glorious past, I would like to offer this poem, entitled *Memories* and written during that year for the magazine *Country Endeavour*, which was essentially for the young members of Wistanstow Youth Club (started by Bill Williams), and from where he plucked Mike Powell and Terry Pugh, both of Craven Arms, to assist him at the WVS Boys Camp. The magazine dedicates a whole page to the Camp, so I trust it is acceptable to include the poem here.

The author of this delightful piece was 'A.P. Morgan', who was a member of the youth club, but I'm wondering whether or not he (or she) had any connections to the Camp, because it is about a derelict cottage (maybe Picklescott?).

*Memories*

*From the elm tree tall in the wood nearby*
*Comes the mellow tone of a wood pigeon's cry,*
*The garden brook trickles down, with a sigh,*
*By mist covered cobwebs, a delight to the eye.*
*A white-haired granny by the cottage door,*
*The gnarled old yew tree standing o'er,*
*Beneath it, logs, a bench, and a saw;*
*All these are gone, all are no more.*
*The iron pump and the iron rail gate,*
*A flickering fire in the little black grate,*
*The cottage walls hung with fancy plates,*
*The clematis porch; where she used to wait*
*The small best room where the gramophone stands,*
*The grandfather clock with slow moving hands,*
*And the shiny copper warming pans;*
*These are the things I remember of Gran's.*
*The cottage is now nought but rubble and stone,*
*Gone forever, that snug little home.*
*Now the garden brook must run on alone,*
*But my childhood memories will never be gone.*

How beautiful is that? Thank you, A.P. Morgan.

The now late Mr Roy Williams was a very good friend of Bill Williams. His nickname, as any of you who are familiar with my books will know, was "Butcher". I believe it came about as a result of Skipper telling the boys (in jest) that he was a retired wrestler.

Roy was a very likeable (and game) helper on Camp, and had been so almost from the word go. His duties were confined to the kitchen, where he could be found ably assisting Mrs Hull, Mrs Hazlehurst, Mrs Mansell, Pat Irving, or even his wife Di. Indeed, Di and Roy were the cooks when I skippered the Camp for the first time in 1979.

During one of the early 1960s Camps, two of the lads made some interesting notes about Roy's military career after "interviewing" him. My guess is that they decided to ask him about his life in order to do a "piece" at the Campfire, on behalf of their tent group, because at the top of the first page it says:

***A Report on Mr Roy Williams by J. Murphy, D. Mahon and Co.***

Roy was very obliging, as you will discover below. I am quoting the words exactly as either J. Murphy or his "journalistic" fellow tent member D. Mahon wrote them:

*Mr Williams does not live in this county, although he Camps in the county every year.*

*When he was 19 he married the girl next door, who was 18.*

*He is now 39 and has four children, who are Peter 13; Hugh 11; James 5 + 1/2 and Penelope 17.*

*He was in the Royal Navy for several years, and fought in the Second World War. Mr Williams fought in the Battle of Crete in May 1941. The ship was* HMS Kashmir *which was a "Destroyer".*

*On the 20th attack by German dive bombers, they were sunk, because they had no ammo, because of the ship being blown up. One of the bombs got stuck down the funnel which had a disastrous result.*

*When this happened Mr Williams decided, very wisely, to swim, and was picked up by another ship named* HMS Kipling, *after being in the water for six hours!* HMS Kipling *was a Destroyer as well.*

*Before he was in the Navy he was in the Army till 1940, and then he joined the Fleet Air Arm as a pilot but did not pass the test.*

*Every one of Mr Williams' pals got killed. The last to die was Ralph Morris, who went in 1945. He was flying over the Indian Ocean when he went into a dive and was unable to come out of it.*

*Mr Williams spent six years in the Navy during the war, and 20 years altogether, and now he is RNR (Royal Navy Reserve). He retired as a Lieutenant Commander.*

*He is now camping in a lovely country setting on his holidays.*

I did some research after reading this because if it was all true, Roy must have been some years older than Bill, who was born in 1926.

I discovered that *HMS Kashmir* was a destroyer; was in fact sunk on 23rd May 1941, as was *HMS Kelly*. And *HMS Kipling* did pick up some survivors. I can't verify, for a fact the claim that Roy was on either ship... but it's a bit of a tall tale if he wasn't!

Roy Williams had an outstanding and distinguished military career, ending it as the lads tell us above (and it's a fact) as a Lt Commander in the Royal Navy.

He wasn't a bad poet either! When we moved to our new and permanent premises (1980); a field sold to Bill by the Davies brothers of Minton Batch, it rained and rained and rained! We moved everyone who was sleeping in the tents on the front of the field into the newly acquired "hall". It was in fact a former RAF dormitory; nevertheless, it was also a godsend.

Roy wrote the following light-hearted words in recognition of the problem the rain had caused us:

*They built a huge hut at the new Longmynd Camp*
*No rain on the tables, they weren't even damp.*
*But on the third day, when it rained cats and dogs,*
*We found that the tents had turned into the bogs!*
*Skipper dear, I'm cold and I'm damp,*
*Oh please send me home from this terrible Camp.*
*The lady in the cookhouse is working all day,*

*She never gets out to sleep, or even to play.*
*She's married to "Butcher", and her name it is Di,*
*When Skipper complained, he got a black eye!*
*Tomorrow's the last day, I'm happy to say,*
*I've never before hoped for a happier day.*
*So if I am good, and Mum says I'm a dear*
*Perhaps I won't have to come back...*
*Till next year!!*

Very tongue-in-cheek. No-one got cold and damp, we moved everyone into the hall when it was obvious the tents weren't holding the heavy rain back.

It's "Butcher" I have to thank for giving me my favourite hymn. Being an old "sea dog", he could be always heard singing or whistling around the kitchen, *For Those in Peril on the Sea*.

I grew to love this hymn, and it is still my absolute favourite to this day; I'm always singing the words, or humming the tune. I suppose it took Roy back to the sinking of *HMS Kashmir*, when he was without doubt in peril on the sea... if his "interview" was factual and correct... and I personally have no reason to assume otherwise! It is a favourite of America too, coincidentally.

My brother Billy was included in selection for the 1964 Camp, as was John Preece; both newcomers to this wonderful paradise. They were allocated to the same tent (3), and quickly became friends, as they knew each other from living in Low Hill. These days, John (and Kenny Turner) are my best friends, with the exception of my sons, Marc and Tom. Readers of my previous books will be familiar with both John and Kenny and, obviously, my boys.

The full list of Skipper's 1964 Camp:

Tent One: Arthur Maguire, Patrick Maguire, Francis Maguire, Colin Bradley, Robert Bradley.
Tent Two: Stephen Jarvis, Nigel Jarvis, Lawrence Morroll, David Hogg.
Tent Three: John Preece, Graham Russell, Nigel Ordinans, Nicholas Ordinans, Billy Scriven.
Tent Four: Tom Badger, Keith Giles, Keith Barnes, John Brace, Philip Hayes.
Tent Five: Leslie Spring, Jimmy Simpson, Melvin Doherty, Tim Cottle.
Tent Six: Sargy Chand, Sarwen Chand, David Twiss, Stephen Tranter, Edwin Tranter.

I would love to think some of the lads mentioned above, and throughout this book, are seeing their names in print on the pages of this final instalment of my trilogy on this fantastic place! And of course there are many more lads and staff members mentioned in my previous books.

Bill's voluntary staff for 1964 was made up of the following "diamonds": Mr R. ("Butcher") Williams, Mr B. Minton-Beddoes,

Mr P.J. Carter, Mr R. Lewis, Mr M. Bowen, Mrs W. Hull (the WVS stalwart who cooked for the whole Camp for many years, this year she was assisted by Mr J. Birch), Mr E. Williams, Mr J. Cully, Mr P. Williams (Roy's son), and Mr B. Jones.

This was the only year in *our* Camp's entire forty-year history that one lad (Jimmy Simpson) won both the Best Camper and Best Cook awards; with Arthur Maguire securing second place in both categories! Well done, lads.

The 1964 programme informs us that a fancy dress competition was held on the first Sunday. In all my years at Camp, this "crazy hour" was saved until just before the Campfire, on the second and last Sunday. Abolishing this "farce" was one of only a couple of changes I made to the programme when I became Skipper. I think now, however, I might have retained it, had it been held on the first Sunday.

I wasn't a fan of the fancy dress; it was a nightmare for the tent leaders, who not only had to sort out a "costume" of sorts (from very limited resources) for everyone in their tent to wear, but then get the tent "ship shape" for a snap tent inspection immediately afterwards! Usually, at this particular inspection, the tents were in "shit order"!

Sarwen Chand won the competition in 1964 as "The National Health Witch Doctor from Minton". In second place came Francis Maguire as a "Fisherman", with David "Monster" Hogg in third, for his portrayal of a "Tramp"; in fourth place came Leslie Spring, who explained to everyone: 'I'm a Zulu Polo.'

On page ten of the *Camp Magazine*, Francis Maguire took it upon himself to give his opinion of the tents and their members:

*Tent One: (Francis's) Tent one has got one or two "skivers" but on the whole (in games and other activities) the tent is quite good.*

*Tent Two: They have only got four in their tent. But the only one that tries is David Hogg. The other three just don't bother.*

*Tent Three: This tent is good for workers in tent competitions. Everyone tries hard.*

*Tent Four: Not so good as Tent Three in anything, and one or two are cheeky, and skivers. The only two who try are Tom Badger and John Brace.*

*Tent Five: A good tent for cooks, games and competitions, although they have had one or two sick.*

*Tent Six: A good tent for inspections and games.*

Thanks for that, Francis!

My turn came in 1965, and it's a well-known fact that I couldn't stand the place at first. I hated being away from my mom, and the vast openness of the countryside... but I quickly grew to love it, and how!

Trevor Davis (mentioned above) had now become a full member of staff, in charge of Tent Six. So effectively, he was the first "beneficiary" to offer his assistance to Bill as a helper.

It was a pity he didn't stay longer, as I remember him being a good leader.

Our tent leader (we were assigned to Tent Four, the bell tent) was Hugh Williams. I told the sad story (in my earlier book) of Hugh not ever coming back to Camp again after being involved in an accident with one of the lads. The lad in question was Stephen Carter. I haven't named him previously, and I only do so now because the unfortunate circumstances of the accident were, believe it or not, included in a poem (of sorts) published in the *Camp Magazine* by a "mystery author" who managed - he said - to name every single lad on that Camp of 1965:

*Should you ask me whence these verses, whence these names that each mean people*
*I should answer, I should tell you, from the Camp that stood at Minton,*
*Clustered tents upon the hillside, on the hillside which turned to mudslide*
*When the rainstorms beat down on Minton*
*Who's this peering out of Tent Three? It's Johnnie Preece and all his tent mates, proudly boasting theirs is top tent.*
*Fancy seeing both the Bradleys, third time here and still surviving*
*More than poor old Stephen Carter; stood too close and copped it proper!*
*Not like Jim O'Neil and Tommy, keeping clear of work and*

*working, only busy being bolshy, whilst the others won the prizes.*
*Richard Hill, the finest cook prize: Derek Clarke the prize for Camping, and Billy Scriven won the mag' comp'.*
*Nigel Jarvis, junior sportsman; not overlooking elder sportsman, Francis Maguire*
*Nor his brother, sweet voiced Patrick, singing to us at the Campfire with another singer;*
*Malcolm Cooke with golden voice box, even noisy Graham listened, and the "Monster" brothers Hogg.*
*Yes David and Terry, and Ginger Evans. All were there with "Boxer Topping"*
*Stephen Tranter, Alan Scriven; fearless runners, fast and long.*
*Even Michael, discus thrower, stirred himself and came to life.*
*When the Campers gathered closer, closer to the flaming Campfire,*
*Where the flames leapt, even brighter lighting up our grubby faces.*
*Gathered round it through the evening; plucky Tony, batsman George and quiet Stephen*
*Leaping up like young John Topping when he won the junior high jump*
*Yes he won the high jump on the sports field, that small sports field close to Minton.*

*So the Campfire slowly burnt out, burnt to a heap of smouldering ashes*
*So we turned our faces homeward...*
*Who's for coming back next year?*

A brilliant effort, but he, like me, could do with taking a leaf from the poetry art of our own Owen J. Lewis.

Tent three (Colin Bradley, Robert Bradley, Francis Maguire, Patrick Maguire and John Preece) won the Tent Marks competition.

The total expenditure for Camp '65 was £166 11s 11d, excluding money spent on outings, and there were a few! It's important to mention, however, that every tent group didn't go on every outing. It was usually decided by position in the tent marks competition, etc., unless we were going somewhere that included all of us, like the seaside, and cinema.

Included on the expenses list was the Boultons coach we travelled to Borth in. That cost the Camp coffers £18 0s 0d.

Petrol and diesel came to £6 3s 7d and the total cost of gas used amounted to £7 18s 0d.

Surprisingly, the marquee came at a cost of £9 5s 0d. I was of the opinion, throughout the years we used it, that the company who supplied the marquee, Beddoes, loaned it to Bill for free.

Another interesting expense was £2 14s 6d, which was the total amount paid out to some of the staff as travel costs. When my time as a member of staff arrived, I never claimed a single penny in expenses, for anything during all my years as a part of the staff. Cash spent on other outings besides the seaside totalled £12 7s 9d. It was money well spent, on: the cinema; swimming baths; Ludlow Castle, and fish and chips followed by ice cream for everyone.

The annual Camps led by Skipper Bill Williams sailed on with no fuss and moderate progress. As stated in my first book, I was chosen as Best Camper in 1967, my last full Camp as one of "Bill's Boys". Below, I list a few excerpts from the letter I wrote to Skipper shortly after arriving back home:

*Dear Skip*

*Got home alright, and my brothers and "Gorgeous"* too.*

*Cyril's parents weren't there to meet him off the coach, so he had to walk to Fordhouses, and that's a pretty long walk from town, especially with his case to carry!*

*When I told my mom I had been chosen as 'Best Camper' she said "Well done, I thought you'd never do it." But I had faith all along that I stood a good chance. I volunteered to fetch water and wood when it wasn't our tent's turn to do it. And I helped around the site whenever the opportunity arose. Thank you for noticing that Skip'.*

*When you were giving out the prizes at Campfire, you said "And the Best Camper..."*

*I was thinking that this was my last chance. Then you said my name. I was over the moon as I wanted a lasting memory of you and such a wonderful place.*

*Thank you very much indeed Skipper, and I hope with all my heart, that I see you again sometime.*

*All the best*

*Alan Scriven (Tent Six)*

*"Gorgeous" was the nickname of George Murray. He was a friend, and a neighbour from Fifth Avenue. There's a somewhat harrowing tale concerning George and me on a day out on the Long Mynd, in the early pages of my first book.

I'd had my fourteenth birthday, so I knew that the chances of me going to Camp again were, in the very least, slim. After that letter had been assigned to the post-box I thought, *That's it, I'll never see that again, or the Camp, and worst of all; Skipper!* But I was wrong on all counts.

# Chapter Five

When I told Bill Williams of my plan to write a book on the history of the Longmynd Adventure Camp, he was very supportive. When he very kindly gave me "valuable" documents that he had saved, amongst them were all the letters he had received from lads from across the years. I was delighted to see my own amongst them. Bill had kept everything, as I did. I could never have written such a concise history of the Camp without his kind gift.

I dedicated my (first) book to Bill's memory.

I must also thank Pete Roberts (whose Camp origins are featured - in his own words - in my second book) for his gift of Minton Camp 1967 magazine. Pete was our group's tent leader for my last Camp as a beneficiary. I respected him, and thought very highly of him, as I do to this day. We are back in contact now, and I am delighted that we are!

During the springtime of 1968, my younger brother David was looking forward to receiving a letter from Mrs Lathe of Wolverhampton WRVS, confirming his selection for Camp that year. When the letter arrived, however, I was surprised and more than a little overwhelmed to discover that my name was included too. I would have had my fifteenth birthday by the time Camp rolled round again; making me above the age limit. I didn't realise this, however, until Skipper informed me at Camp on Sports Day.

This part of my Camp history is well documented in my first two books.

All I will say here is: I began my holiday at Camp in 1968 as one of the beneficiaries, and ended it as a junior member of staff. I was over the moon!

For the final Camp of the "swinging sixties", I was invited along to continue what I had started halfway through the previous year's Camp. I was to be on the staff, but not (as yet) in the capacity of tent leader; that responsibility wouldn't come until the following year.

I felt unbelievably lucky that Skipper was willing to give me an opportunity to be a good and responsible member of his team for a whole Camp. And although my duties only amounted to those of a "bottom of the ladder gofer", or "Dogsbody", I gave one hundred per cent every time I was assigned a task. The majority of my daytime work was taken up assisting various tent leaders with whatever they were doing with their lads. The downside of this (without being disrespectful to our late Skipper) was that I would be assigned to a different group almost every day, so I underwent some repetition... but I was at Camp, and this fact in itself was a massive bonus!

A few details of the 1968 expenditure:

Sweets £4 18s 0d

Bread (4) £6s 6d

Stamps 7s 0d

Paraffin (total) £1 1s 9d

Bacon ££2 8s 0d

Phone calls £1 0s 0d

Observer Books (prizes) £3 10s 0d

The donations included a very substantial (for the times) £10 0s 0d from someone who wanted to remain anonymous. Plus: Peter Williams (staff) £1 0s 0d; Cyril Gausden (staff) 10s 0d; Mrs Pat Hazlehurst £1 1s 0d; Miss "Swinny" Swinnerton (friend of Pat) £1 0s 0d.

There were always donations of another sort each year, i.e. foodstuff or free (or reduced fees) entry to various places of interest. And, of course, our beloved cow-truck!

Actually, I wasn't the only former beneficiary to be invited to be a junior staff member in 1969. A good friend of mine (now sadly deceased), Terry Hogg, also came to Camp. Terry could only manage three days, however, due to work commitments. But he gave what time and assistance he could, and Bill was very grateful, as he always was for everyone's help.

I had travelled to Camp on the Don Everall coach with the lads. The Wolves boys boarded at Faulkland Street Coach Park (still in use today) and joined the "Brummie" lads for the usual noisy but well-behaved journey. I am not saying there were never any scuffles or fall-outs between us and the Brummies, but it was exceptionally rare. We all, for the most time, got on really well, and even more so upon our arrival at Camp. Well, no one wanted to upset the big copper!

On the final morning of Camp, whilst everyone was basically involved with their own thing (because the clean-up proper couldn't begin until the lads had left for home), the Skipper called me to one side. He said that if I wanted to, I could stay behind to help with "breaking Camp". Reading my mind, he added, 'I'll give you a lift home if you can stay and help me.'

I didn't have to consider it. There was no possibility of me refusing; it was the least I could do. So, after responding in the affirmative, I ran off to find my brother: 'Dave, I'm not coming back with you, I'm staying here to help with the cleaning up; tell Mom when you get back. Skipper's bringing me home.'

'Can I stay back as well then, Al?'

'No. How can you when someone's got to let Mom know?'

'We can ask George (Murray) to tell her,' David persisted.

'No Dave, you're going back on the coach.'

And that's how it played out. I finally arrived at home around 6pm. Skipper met my mother, and they chatted for what seemed like ages; most of their conversation revolving around Camp, obviously. It was also an unexpected opportunity for my elder brother Billy to see Skipper again. What a kind thing for

Bill to do; and it wasn't just because he was short in numbers for help with the clear-up operation, I'm sure... because he repeated the gesture on more than one occasion as the years unfolded.

I was a little surprised, incidentally, to learn (from Skipper) that "breaking" and "striking" Camp both had the same meaning... apparently.

Another lad who had outgrown his beneficiary status was Ian "Scottie" Gibbons. Scottie was, like me, a Wolverhampton lad. He lived at 85 Vicarage Road with his family and, like me, joined Bill's merry band of voluntary helpers. Scottie and I are friends again now, and I am very happy to be so. We are members of a group of former LAC personnel from across the decades, which I formed a couple of years ago, to celebrate - in our own special way - the sixtieth anniversary of the Camp, because sadly we never got to celebrate its ruby anniversary, and as far as I am aware, no anniversary has been celebrated since!

Obviously, most of us had lost touch with each other over the years we were at Camp and the publication of my first book. The book, however, reached the people who now form our group. Not all members attend our monthly get togethers, but they are equally valued members just the same.

Scottie was working for our National Health Service at the time of his recent retirement. But in July 2020 when he, his lovely wife Carol, and other members of our newly formed group (which we call “Minton Memories”) joined me in the field some of us were camping in for my birthday week, he gave me a complete run down of his whole working career... and it was fascinating to hear how it had gone. From leaving school at the same time that I had, Scottie has worked in many jobs in many countries to earn a crust; he is also an accomplished radio presenter... as is/was another of our group, one Owen J. Lewis Esq.

Ian lives in Howarden, North Wales, with Carol, and their pet dog Zeke. He is (as I write) awaiting a call to return to the front line to assist the NHS as it battles – under severe pressure – to halt the aggressive march of Covid 19.

I forgot to mention Ian “Scottie” Gibbons when I wrote my thank you list at the end of my first book. So may I correct that oversight now: thank you very much, Scottie, for all the valued assistance you kindly gave to Bill, and the Longmynd Adventure Camp.

# Chapter Six

The new decade opened with a change in the law with regard to the "Age of Majority" being reduced from twenty-one to eighteen years of age, on 1st January 1970.

Other UK events of that year included the end of the half crown as legal tender, and the introduction of the Range Rover.

The National Westminster Bank was "born", with the amalgamation of the National Provincial Bank and the Westminster Bank.

On 22nd January, a Boeing 747 safely landed at London's Heathrow Airport; the first jumbo jet to do so.

The Prince of Wales joined the Royal Navy on 19th February.

On 2nd March 1970, the Rhodesian Prime Minister declared the country a republic, thereby breaking all ties with the British Crown

Everton won the First Division title; Chelsea won the F.A. Cup for the first time, and Jack Nicklaus won the Open Golf Championship.

Paul McCartney announced he had left The Beatles.

The Conservatives won the General Election with a majority of just thirty seats.

15th October marked the last journey of barges hauling long-distance goods commercially on Britain's canals.

The first "Page 3 girl" appeared in the *Sun* newspaper (my turn on page 7 didn't come till the middle eighties).

Nijinsky became the first horse to win The English Triple Crown.

In other news: yours truly was asked to be a tent leader by the Skipper of the LAC. I accepted the invitation with gratitude for the trust invested in me.

I travelled by train to Shrewsbury on the Thursday morning, and was met by Bill, who took me to Camp after we did a little shopping. The main shopping for the Camp was done by Bill, and Francis Rudge, later; we just picked up a few things on our way to Camp. Upon arrival (we were second to arrive after Mr Rudge), there wasn't much to do because we had to wait for a few more members of staff before we could get cracking properly. Eventually, I was assigned to help with erecting the tents. I grew to enjoy this task over the years, and the company of whoever was asked to work with me; we always had a laugh as we got stuck into the job. The other helpers on that Thursday included Mick Powell, Peter Walker, Pete Roberts, Brian Irving, and Arthur Drew.

During that particular Camp, I was asked to play one of the "ghosts of Minton Batch" opposite Skipper's nephew, (the now late) John Clarke. Again, this escapade - and that's being conservative - is told in detail in my first book. John was a great guy, I liked him a lot. It was a sad day for his family, and the Camp, when he passed away suddenly from an aneurism.

The Camp of 1970 passed without any major incident... well, you couldn't say the ghost hunting night was a major incident... no, it was fun, in the end... after the Skipper calmed down!

1971 Camp came and went without much ado.

I was working at Carvers, the well-known builders and plumbers merchants of Wolverhampton. I had progressed in my career there to a position on the trade counter, under John "Ginger" Brown. So, as it has turned out, the first and last jobs of my working life saw me working for a boss called Brown.

The details of Camp 1972 are a little vague, due to not many documents being available. But for me it was another success, and I felt very comfortable as I grew into my duty to the Skipper, and my responsibilities to my charges.

I have the list of boys who attended the 1973 Camp, thanks to a homemade (or Camp-made) card we all signed as a thank you to Mr Pat Greenhous (a Shrewsbury businessman, and friend of the Camp), who lived in Little Stretton.

Mr Greenhous had kindly allowed us use of his garden pool for swimming sessions. SBill thought a card from us, and made by us, would be a nice thank you. Exactly why it is in my possession, I'm sorry I haven't a clue!

Tent One: Leader John Walker. Paul Singh, Paul Berrill, Alan White, Kevin White, Donald Connelly.

Tent Two: Leader John Clarke. Steven Carless, Martyn Carless, Michael Healey, John Healey, Ian Thomas.

Tent Three: Leader Alan Scriven. Steven Evans, Satpal Singh, Freddie Evans, Dennis Nicholls, Tommy Simpkiss, Nicky Gibbons (younger brother of Ian "Scottie" Gibbons).
Tent Four: Leader Eric Bullion. Errol Ellis, Winston Ellis, Theodore Johnson, Paul Stanton, Shaun Healey.
Tent Five: Leader (unreadable). R. Weaver, M. Lockyer, P. Williams, B. Lockyer, K. Weaver.
Tent Six: Leader (unreadable). Jimmy Simpkiss, John Benn, Peter Howard, Terry Simpkiss, Stephen Pursell, Gary Beardsmore.

The card was decorated on the front with sketches of the rope slide we had erected that year; a very ghostly-looking "angel of the Camp", and a figure of a person chasing a sleep-walker... at least, that's what it looks like to me!

The dedication reads:

*To Mr Pat Greenhous*

*This is a small token of our appreciation of your kind generosity towards the boys of the WRVS Camp.*

How nice: thank you very much, Mr Greenhous.

Jimmy and Terry Simpkiss of Tent Six had been part of my first ever group as a tent leader in 1970, along with their brother Tommy, who elected to join me again in Tent Three.

Below is a piece which was written by a lady for whom I held a very high regard, and who became a valued friend as early as the middle sixties; former West Mercia Police Superintendent Pat Hazlehurst QPM. Readers of my previous books will be very familiar with Pat. She was, in every sense of the word, a Camp icon. Pat was very closely involved with the Camp for almost three decades.

I feel it is worthwhile including it in this book because it is essentially a Q&A sheet which I considered the reader might find interesting; the viewpoint of another person who was a major "player" in the growth and prosperity of the charity.

It wasn't actually dated, but the title "Longmynd Boys Camp 1970s" gives us a definite hint of the charity's position (at that time) through Pat's eyes:

*<u>What is the Camp?</u>*

*It is a Camp for about 40 boys aged 11 to 15yrs. It is held annually for ten days in August, on the Longmynd hills. The boys sleep in tents, which are used as a kitchen; staffroom, and storage throughout the year. All the equipment, including the hut and cooking facilities and utensils, was purchased with money raised by an appeal, locally in Shropshire, some ten years or so ago.*

*Who are the Boys who use it?*

*The boys come under the canopy of "Under-Privileged" and hail from Wolverhampton and Birmingham. They are selected by the WRVS after various organisations i.e. NSPCC; Social Services; Probation Service; Hospital Almoners etc, recommend boys for a holiday. The WRVS then place them, either at our Camp, or in private homes. The majority of boys selected have never had a holiday prior to coming to Camp. The WRVS sponsor each child, and even arrange medicals, provision of suitable clothing, if required, and transport to and from Camp.*

*Who are the Camp staff?*

*Once the boys arrive at Camp, they become the responsibility of a group of people, under the leadership of the Skipper. Many of the staff are giving up all or at least a large proportion of their annual holidays from work; very often repeating this year after year. The staff members come from many different walks of life, including policeman, cadet, forestry worker, clergy, doctor, engineer, trainee miner, teacher, student, sales rep', soldier, postman, and even some former boys of the Camp who have returned to 'give something back', as it were.*

*The principle is that the staff member (tent leader) eats, sleeps, and lives with his group for the duration of the Camp. We hope, and believe that in this way, each group becomes a happy "family unit". All members of staff are unpaid volunteers which in itself is remarkable when one considers the amount of money that they spend during the time they are at Camp. And the majority do not claim even their travel expenses.*

*<u>What do we do at Camp?</u>*

*The main object is to ensure that it is a holiday worth remembering. I think this is certainly the case, just by the number of boys who return year after year; and the tears when it's time to go home. And it's worth saying that a lot of them have never been away from home before, let alone basic Camping in a field far from their home.*

*Discipline can sometimes (very rarely) be a problem, but over the years we have overcome this, by and large. In fact the standard these days is extremely higher than one might imagine, given the fact that they are for the most part, a group of strangers, initially.*

*Most of the time is spent outdoors on the hills and in the valleys. We play a lot of "scout type" games which the lads thoroughly enjoy. Various competitions are held, including a Sports Day; swimming; litter picking, and of course the tent marks "championship" (which considerably helps with the discipline aspect). A day trip to the seaside is also included in our busy programme.*

*We hold a short "religious service" (for those who wish to take part) on each Sunday morning, and a Campfire is held on the final evening of Camp, during which the boys entertain our guests for much coveted tent marks. At the end of the evening, prizes are given out by the Skipper to all those who have won one for various achievements over the Camp period i.e. Best Cook; Best Sportsman, and much sought after "Best Camper", to name a few.*

*Country life, its animals and birds are new to many, and we try to encourage appreciation of all that this entails.*

*Whatever the State, and/or other organisations give the families; no-one can ensure the children actually benefit; we feel however, that our Camp gives the lads that come to us, something no-one can take away: a good holiday where they are cared for by honest people who ask for nothing in return... not even a "thank-you" (which we, and the WRVS always ensure they receive).*

*<u>History of the Camp:</u>*

*The first Camp (proper) was held in 1959, and has been held without exception each year since. The local people have, over the years, been extremely generous with gifts of cash; and kind. All the money that is donated is used for purchasing our own equipment, as in the beginning we were heavily dependent on the kindness of people to lend us stuff we needed. Any spare cash at Camp is spent on prizes; pocket money (if anyone arrives without any), and other special treats. This money is kept in a different account from the day to day Camp fund.*

*It is hoped, eventually, to be able to extend the Camp, to cater for more boys*.*

*Our present site is very generously rented to us for a meagre sum, but this agreement expires soon; therefore our continued progress depends on either securing a renewal of this agreement, or possibly purchasing this field, or another elsewhere if that can't be achieved.*

As far as 1975 is concerned, the only new information I have is the list of people Bill wanted to thank for their help and generosity during the ten days. His well-thought-out list totals thirty-one people, and organisations, etc., some of which I have included in my first book. I think it's perhaps in order to list a few more here. My apologies to those not mentioned below; please be assured, however, of our sincere gratitude, as ever was the case:

Pat Greenhous: Use of pool; £50 donation; truck.
Eric Young: £50 donation.
Mrs Willis of Minton: Cakes.
The Wayside pub, Marshbrook (now the Station pub): Crisps.
Harold Edworthy: 30lbs beef
Mr Chidley (Bottle and Glass pub): Water cart.
The Green Dragon pub: First Night Party.
Noel Morgan: £5 donation.
Miss Saltonstall and Miss Wilkes (Alma St, Shrewsbury): £5 donation.
Betty Goolding: Crisps and Sweets.
Mr & Mrs Brian Irving (Church Stretton, helpers on Camp): Eggs.

When it came to saying thank you, Bill forgot no one, or at least tried not to. Every year, we received some large and small donations, which he considered, quite rightly, were equally vital to the lads' comfort, and also to the continuation of the Camps.

As a small token of his gratitude, Bill always tried to remember all the people who had helped the Camp on its journey through the decades, when it came to invitations to either first-night parties or any special events during the course of his ten-day Camps.

In 1976 and 1977, Bill's lists included the committee (formed in 1976), as well as the following:

Wilde's of Dorrington (for loan of generator)
Percy and F. Prince (Farmers of Little Stretton)
Jack Williams
Mr and Mrs Challinor, and their daughter Carol
Ned, Cliff and Dave Davies
Diane Garmston (WRVS)
Alf Sankey
The Royal Observer Corps
Dorothy Davies (Shrewsbury Chronicle)
E.J.M. Green (Vice Chair Church Stretton Parish Council)
Jasper Moore MP
Mrs G.M. Hazlerigg (WRVS Children's Holiday Chief Organiser)
M.J. Hartley (Church Stretton Round Table)

The Camps rolled on. The late seventies saw much progress with regard to the number of lads invited to spend time with us. I was a first-choice tent leader by the middle seventies, and fast becoming an ever-present member of the field staff. I enjoyed my years as a tent leader, and would have been very happy to continue, had it not been for an unexpected twist of fate which meant me taking overall charge in 1979, and then from the following year I accepted the responsibility, and the privilege, of becoming the Skipper's trusted number two. All the details are covered in my first book.

What I will always remember about 1979 is the total and unswerving support of the volunteers of that year who joined me, and helped me to be successful in making the Camp a rip-roaring success for the lads who shared it with us. Thank you, and God bless you all.

A lad I well remember from the first Camp of 1980 is Ronnie Edwards. Ronnie, like me, had one of his ears pierced, and he constantly reminded me of the values of turning the sleeper "round and round so it don't stick". Bless you, Ronnie; I hope life's been kind to you.

I mentioned in my first book that we camped on our new site for the very first time in 1980, and that we got washed out of our tents by the rain! Not to worry, however; Ronnie and the rest of us ran to the safety of our new hall.

Bill made me his official "number two" at the beginning of

Camp 1980; thus dawned the beginning of a wonderful (for the most part) partnership which lasted for the decade (well, ten years of Camps), until it imploded in spectacular fashion which sadly resulted in Bill cutting all ties with me and his Camp; regaining interest only when it was too late to save it from slipping beneath the surface of a tidal wave of devastating change!

Due to the fact that the back field on our new site needed to be sown, we were back on Mr Brian Jones's field in 1981; the very same field as was used in 1962.

My senior position was confirmed with an "official title". From this point and onwards, Skipper's second-in-command would hold the title of "Bosun". I absolutely loved my time in this position, until it became almost intolerable in the latter part of the decade, due to being usurped at every opportunity (detailed in my first book).

Skipper's speech during the first-night party on Thursday 28th July 1982 offered one or two interesting facts and figures. He told us that it was the twenty-fourth year of the Camp's existence, in which time there had been a total of thirty-one Camps (we were well into the practice of two Camps per year by this time). He added that his estimate of the number of children who had thus far experienced the delights of this fantastic "oasis" was 1,400... staggering! And I'm so happy to count myself among that number, as I know Scottie and John Preece are, as well as our old pal Len Badger and his brothers. Len lives in Bushbury as I write, and is also happily retired, and a member of our Minton Memories group, as is John, who came to Camp ahead of his brothers, (the late) Alan, and Keith.

Bill also spoke about the cost of Camp, and reminded everyone that the lads were here for a holiday, and therefore every penny spent was justified.

He thanked everyone present, and all the good and kind people of the past who had helped get the Camp to where it was at that moment in time.

Finally, Bill thanked the staff, and I was the first person he mentioned. Looking back, it was due, probably, to me running the 1979 Camp, as a result of Bill's sudden and unfortunate illness, and then acting as his number two in 1980, before my promotion was made permanent in 1981.

Other facts and figures for the two Camps of 1982 include:

Donations of £244.17. This figure included sums kindly given by Mr and Mrs B. Willis of Minton, Mrs Tonks (Walsall WRVS), Cliff Harris (ex-West Mercia Police, friend and colleague of Bill. Cliff also served on the committee for a time), Frank Powell-Bevan, G.T. Grindley (and I. Jones), and lastly, Henry Minkley.

The largest addition to the coffers came via a very welcome £107.37, which was the final total from the first night's buffet draw.

Some of that money, and of course the WRVS sponsorship, together with the cash from Shropshire County Council (for the Shropshire boys) was spent on:

“Friday lunches”. On the day of the lads’ arrival, the staff usually had a spot of lunch in the Wayside Inn, before the coach arrived.

Expenses paid to tent leader Phil Pinniger. Phil (at the time, husband of Joanna Roundell-Greene, who I mentioned earlier) had taken his group to Stokesay Castle for a great day out.

By far, however, the majority of the money was spent on food. John Preece was the Camp cook (from 1981), and although he worked wonders putting on very good meals every single day (except seaside day) for everyone on Camp, most of the cash went on that delicious fact!

Bill had mentioned to me that he was struggling for a cook for that year’s Camps. Being not only a former beneficiary of the Camp, but also a friend and a qualified butcher and chef, I suggested John to Bill. I had in fact already put it to John, and he responded very positively. Bill agreed to give him a shot at it, and was very glad he did. Well, all except for one year when Bill made the decision to “try someone else”. That turned out to be a mistake, so John to his credit, agreed to return in 1985.

John changed the way the kitchen had hitherto been managed, in that he insisted on having a team of assistants (as you see above). Neither Bill, nor I (later) had a problem with this, even though it was "more mouths to feed", as our Skipper so eloquently put it. As Bosun, I was happy with the arrangement because John was able to leave the kitchen for a few hours each day (as were his team), in the safe knowledge that everything had been prepared for the main evening meal. And John being free of the kitchen meant that he and I could spend some time together off Camp. It didn't happen every day, because on some occasions Bill would ask me to accompany him on whatever business he was committed to.

Another reason for John asking for a couple of assistants was his ongoing health problem. He won't mind me telling you, reader, that from the age of twenty-four he has suffered from serious heart problems, and everything that comes with that most dangerous of health issues. To this day, I accompany him to Papworth Heart Hospital in Cambridgeshire every three months for a "Ganglion Block" pain-killing procedure, for which he holds the world record for the number of injections. The man is literally a walking miracle.

I have the results sheet for the first Camp Sports Day. As I said in my first book, it was a work of art how well the field was prepared to include all the events: 100m; 200m; 400m; Relay; Welly-Wang; Discus (I still have both of the original discuses); Sack Race; Javelin; Three-Legged Race, and Obstacle Race.

Sports Day was operated by an age category policy: "Over 12s" and "12 and under".

Here are the results. Is your name among those mentioned? **Over 12:** 100m D. Cox; 200m M. Powell; 400m T. Harris. Welly-Wang Marcus Beezer. Discus T. Harris; Sack T. Harris; Javelin D. Cox; Obstacle M. Powell.

12 and Under: 100m D. Spratt; 200m D. Spratt; 400m A. Scarlett; Welly-Wang J. Chalmers; Discus R. Edwards; Sack A. Scarlett; Javelin J. Chalmers; Obstacle N. Hill.

The relay teams comprised of a mix of both age groups:

Tent One: N. Williams, J. Robinson, J. Cox, J. Felton

Tent Two: R. Fitzpatrick, R. Edwards, A. McGough, D. Jones

Tent Three: M. Powell, A. Scarlett, J. Scarlett, T. Harris

Tent Four: P. Price, C. Blakeman, E. Blakeman, C. Price

Tent Five: G. Singh, D. Rowles, P. Hadlington, S. Bryan

Tent Six: S. Cullen, D. Spratt, I. Keown, L. Toon

Tent Seven: J. Duffy, P. Scarry, P. James, J. Chalmers

Tent Eight: P. Price, J. Kirkham, I. Bash, P. Titley

First past the winning post was Tent Three, with second place being claimed by Tent Six.

The occasions that warranted using eight tents were rare, but on this occasion we had a batch of lads from Shropshire. It proved, I suppose, that the Camp was being recognised more as an outlet for kids from other areas, as well the West Midlands.

And Bill was never a person to say no if asked to accept extra numbers. As long as he was happy that we had the amenities to care for a growing number of lads, that's all that mattered. And why not? The fact that the Camp was at full capacity meant, in a word, success.

As I say above, in 1982 we were back on our own land, having once more relied on the charitable D.O. Jones for the previous year. Bill decided that our field needed urgent attention before we could consider pitching tents on it again. His plan worked; we never again had to resort to bedding the entire Camp down in the hall (as told in my previous books).

And finally, in 1982, Tina gave birth (with me at her side) to our second and last child... our son Thomas, or Tom as he is now known, on 31st July, at 12 noon exactly. Tom's arrival couldn't have been any more different to that of our first child, Marc. Tom was born full-term, weighing 7lbs 6oz. Marc, however, being Tina's first, and the fact that she suffered from toxaemia, arrived five weeks earlier than he should have, on 12th August 1976, at 07:57am; weighing in at just 5lbs 1oz. He had to spend the first ten days of his life in hospital, as he was jaundiced. He also had to make up the weight he'd lost since being born. The good thing is, however, both celebrated their birthdays whilst Camp was in operation.

The following year heralded the charity's silver jubilee and we celebrated with an Open Day. I give details of this in my first book, so I would just like to include a poem I wrote in celebration of our (Bill's) achievement. Notice that it is an acrostic poem, as was my 1977 poem about Bill Williams (see book one):

*Twice ten and five more years our beloved Camp has stood,*
*Weathering the storms of "infancy", and "early childhood"*
*Exceeding all expectations of the most critical eye;*
*Not wishing to be lifted over the stile, instead*
*Telling everyone; "you go on, I'll catch up in a while".*
*For if you strive to achieve a glorious "end",*
*In God's law, you shall succeed.*
*Varying horizons bring more and more chances*
*Each with its own challenging needs.*
*Yet still we move forward in confident hope,*
*Enveloped in a burning desire,*
*And if the winds of change kindly blow our way*
*Rest assured we will reach our "goal",*
*Spurred on by this historic day!*

I have never professed to be a poet (as you will discover from my previous books, and further into this one), but I enjoy "having a go".

In 1983, I made another attempt at the gruelling "Longmynd Hike". Below is my written record of the day:

*Arriving in good time at Church Stretton School, I wait for my friends just inside the gates. The hike begins at 1300hrs sharp and I am ready for it! The object of the exercise is to get round a fifty-mile course, visiting eighteen checkpoints (even briefly crossing the border into Wales) in a pre-determined sequence, to be completed in a time of twenty-four hours maximum.*

*As soon as my mates join me, we all make our way inside, where our gear is thoroughly examined. Any required item we don't have can be purchased before we are given our "checkpoint cards". These are to be presented at all thirteen checkpoints, where they will be pierced at the particular checkpoint relevant to our progress, thus preventing any temptation to 'duck' one or two of them... as if!?*

*We also have to have, amongst other necessities, an emergency ration, e.g. a couple of bars of chocolate which have to be handed in, unopened, at the end of the hike. Failure to have your emergency rations equals disqualification! A whistle is another essential piece of kit which has to be carried. I am using my "Bosun's Whistle" from Camp.*

*Joining me on the hike are my friends Malcolm Webster, Ian Gray and Mike Jones. Mal' and Ian, alias "Iggle", are colleagues of mine from Camp; Mike is a friend I met some time ago through our Skipper, Bill Williams.*

*In the weeks leading up to the hike, I managed to get some sponsorship, which means that if my effort is successful, I stand to raise the princely sum of £100 for the Camp.*

*It is the first Saturday of October. The hike is always held at this time; not too cold, and certainly not too warm!*

*The sun is shining warmly, however, as we finally make our way to the starting point, all of us got the thumbs up for our gear and attire. Denims are forbidden, as are shorts, and one's footwear has to be hiking boots; I have just recently bought a pair (nearly new) from Bill for twelve pounds. They're strong and heavy, and actually, I'm now wondering whether I should have broken them in a bit more before challenging them to get me through this!*

*The start point is a sea of excitement as people of all ages from teen to pensioner anticipate their own particular challenge. Many will fall by the wayside; I'm just praying I won't be one of the failures... £100 is a lot of money!!!*

*Mike is very confident, and a past master of this most gruesome of tests. I'm so happy he has joined us; he'll keep us going when we start to flag, as we most certainly will. Well we haven't done any training to speak of so it's going to be difficult to say the least!*

*Out of the blue the starting whistle echoes around the school playground, bringing us all to immediate action. Mal who is making his third attempt to get thirteen holes on his check card advises us to "take it easy, no point in rushing". Mike is of a different opinion, though. He thinks we should "step on it" to get the first few checkpoints "under our belt before dark". Hang on Mike, it's only one o'clock!*

*We all make it comfortably to the top of the Lawley hill, our first checkpoint, four miles into the hike. Looking south, I see Caradoc, seemingly within spitting distance... but... it's actually the forty-eight-mile point. Jesus, what have we let ourselves in for? But the panoramic scenery as we stand on top of the Lawley is truly a sight to behold. And the good news is, that with every ascent, and there'll be a fair few the farther we go, the views will just get better. The four of us are old hands at walking the Shropshire hills; I've been doing it for eighteen years now, and Mal, Iggle and Mike are local to the area.*

*We descend the Lawley, and on we toil, over the A49 and onto the Long Mynd proper.* [The eagle-eyed reader will notice Long Mynd as two words whereas our Camp name purposely fuses the two words together (hence my book titles); this was Bill Williams's idea, and I like it... it's different.]

*As our fellow hikers, or some of them, pass us, we offer our good wishes for their success, and they respond in kind. We're going well but it's very early into our task. At t*

*he twelve-mile point, however, I am given a timely reminder that this was never going to be a stroll, or a series of quiet ambling, as a sharp pain sears through my suspect right knee! It has been a problem on and off since the accident in the gym back home. I was involved in a training session with the Sunday league team I was playing for a few years ago, when one of my team-mates clattered into me; our knees colliding full on at speed! I wasn't happy because it was the first training session I had partaken in since an injury to the same knee forced me out of the team for nine weeks!*

*I have stupidly forgotten to pack a knee-strap so am quietly praying that my knee will hold out, as I continue towards Stiperstones, where I hope to get some treatment of sorts in order to carry on. Mike is proving a real pal, a Godsend actually; spurring us all on with words of encouragement straight from the heart.*

*By the time we reach Stiperstones and "Devil's Chair", Mal has fallen victim to a temporary bout of cramp. He's received some treatment, as have I, so we continue on.*

*The sun bids us farewell as we descend the Stiperstones, and soon dusk is a fleeting companion before darkness takes hold. The dark proves no friend; teasing us, and leading us down unfamiliar and false routes, sapping our strength, until our eyes (and our torches) take the strain... and we view our map(s).*

*The pain in my knee is back with a familiar vengeance, and despite more treatment and short spells of rest, my chances of success are diminishing somewhat! I must shake off this pessimistic veil if I am to stand any chance at all of succeeding... but the doubts are coming thick and fast as the miles get longer and longer, all the time sapping our already ebbing strength... well mine, anyway. Mike was proving to be the fittest amongst us.*

*Luckily (I thought) the 22-mile checkpoint is a pub, and we all take advantage, in the form of a couple of pints of beer each and a sandwich. We soldiered on, and it isn't long before we're regretting having the alcohol; a silly mistake I won't make again when next I challenge myself to complete 50 miles in a time of 24 hours. No, the beer is not helping in any way, shape or form.*

*Mal and I could never have guessed that the next checkpoint - Shelve: 27 miles - would be our "breaking point". By now our rucksacks feel like lumps of lead, bearing down on spines growing weaker with every step; our vision almost non-existent as tired eyes fight to stay open. The long lane leading to Shelve checkpoint and first-aid station forces gaps between us, and once I'm walking alone, the dreaded doubts resurface in my muddled head; this is an unforgiving hike and we have abused it by drinking alcohol, and not bringing items that would have assisted us; in my case, my knee strap.*

*Eventually, we all arrive at Shelve. Mike is rearranging his rucksack whilst Iggle is drinking hot soup. Mal is nowhere to be seen but Mike reassures us by explaining that he's in the toilet.*

*I get a drink before delving into my rucksack for yet more sustenance. Looking around, I see lots of fellow hikers; the majority of them look as knackered as I feel. Mike comes over and asks if I'm okay. I'm okay. I'm fit; able and determined to crack this bloody hike! I thought of all the money I was to gain in sponsorship, for our beloved Camp. So yes, I'm continuing, and I am going to succeed. As long as I have Mike with me (us), success is a formality. Not so, however!*

*The "nurse" kindly bandaged both my knees over my brown corduroy trousers, and massaged my knotted calves. I feel better instantly, telling myself that it's only another 23 miles; I had cracked the half of it, and more. As we prepare to move off, Mal suddenly and quite unexpectedly announces his intention to 'retire' from the event, saying, "I just can't muster any more willingness from tired and injured ankles and feet." Essential parts of the body needed to have any hope of success. Naturally, we all tried to coax him into a change of heart, but to no effect, his mind was set. As if forsaking a fallen colleague in the face of an advancing enemy, we reluctantly say our farewells.*

*Mal surrenders his check card to the officials (he'll get it back as a memento, as we all will once back at the school), and his last bar of chocolate to me before walking towards the vehicle that will carry him back to Church Stretton School, where he'll sleep until morning.*

*We set off. Not five hundred yards after leaving the checkpoint, however, an unforeseen pitfall (in the shape of a deep tractor tyre ditch) claims the second member of our group... me! I go over, and fall to my right, cracking my already painful and suspect knee on the rocky surface. The pain is incredible. It is now patently obvious that I cannot possibly go on. I doubt I can do another mile, never mind the 23 that are*

*standing between me and completion of this body and mind tester! So reluctantly, I make my way slowly back to the checkers, and explain my situation. I'm offered mild painkillers, which I'm very grateful for, but continuing is a no-hoper, I'm done for. My knees (right one mainly) are in sh*t order; I can't risk permanent damage. So it's down to Mike and Iggle to get round the course successfully, and I really hope they do. I'm determined to try again next year, but for this year's effort, that's it, 27 miles completed out of a required 50.*

*Mal, seemingly happy with my reappearance, comforts me until the Land Rover is ready to make yet another journey back to Church Stretton School, where we will spend the night.*

Mike and Ian went on to successfully complete the hike. My efforts raised £86, which didn't stop me feeling like a failure; inept and incapable. I made a vow to myself that I would complete the 50-mile Long Mynd hike... and with Mike's help again, I did! Thanks, Mike.

By this time in the Camp's illustrious fairy tale, I was well and truly a part of the senior staff, answering only to our Skipper. My title was Bosun and I was, by and large, respected by most... at least in the presence of the children.

As well as cash from donations, and personal efforts (sponsored walks, etc.), money was coming in from hiring out the premises.

It was very cheap back then to spend a weekend at the Camp (total income from letting was averaging just about £50 p.a.); thankfully quite a few organisations were making full use of its limited facilities. How that situation has changed! The Camp bears little to no resemblance of how it was when we were its beating heart. These days, money, and lots of it, is thrown at it, and is obviously being well spent on the site.

A great deal of very hard work was being done to the Camp back in "our day", on very little cash, and a lot of good will. That fact is not recognised or even remembered today, however. The vast majority of the people who make up today's committee know absolutely nothing about the Camp's glorious past and what went into ensuring that the site was in an acceptable condition year on year, in order for us to hold successive holiday Camps for socially deprived children (who, in its final years of the original Camp, doing what it was created for, came from many parts of the country). The few remaining committee members from back then seemingly choose not to acknowledge historic facts.

Yes, it is true that the website and occasional brochures such as *Dawn Chorus* attempt to offer some "historic information" about the LAC. In my considered opinion (and knowledge), however, I can say that much of it is factually incorrect!

Bill and I worked extremely well together from the moment (at the beginning of the first Camp of 1980) he said that my time as a tent leader was over, and that I was to be his official number two. And no one would have thought that this arrangement would not continue in this vein until Bill decided (himself) to hand over the reins to me.

But fate can be cruel...

# Chapter Seven

As I've said in my previous books, my mother raised my siblings and me without the support of a man, which back in the day was an extremely difficult task. Of course, I had absolutely no idea about my own dad as I grew up.

Her struggle wasn't lost on me; I realised how hard it was for her, and I vowed that when I could, I would repay my mom for what she had given me; given us! She taught us to value money and to respect it. She made us look after what few possessions we had, and not to take anyone else's. I did my bit to repay her for everything she had gone without in order to feed us with what little she had. After I married Tina in 1974, and left home, I continued to pay my mom "board money" (with considerable interest), right up to the month she died.

Actually, she married in 1972, much to my surprise, and that of a few others, too. For a good many years, she had been involved with a man whom I mention a few details about in earlier books. Truth to say, though, the fact that he moved into our house a good while before they tied the knot, helped not one iota towards getting the family out of its poverty status.

My mother had known poverty all her life. She was raised in poverty from the word go. My maternal grandparents had eight children in total. Their second born, Edwin, lived for only a very short time, however, so that left them with just the one son, my uncle Billy; he was the family member who introduced my dad to my mom. And the person I turned to for answers regarding my biological father.

Uncle Billy grew up to become a soldier, joining the Royal Artillery. After leaving the Army, Billy made his life in the London area, driving lorries for a living. He married Beryl Fowler, who was to die early, leaving him with a young daughter, my cousin Susan. Unfortunately, he lost Susan to her maternal grandparents soon after being bereaved. They (I discovered after making contact with Sue's two children, and husband) told my cousin that her father had deserted her! Bill's version of events was in total contrast to his in-laws', however. I made contact with Susan's immediate family via the family history website Ancestry.co.uk but was told that Susan did not want any contact with me, or any member of the Scriven family, following her mother's death. I tried to make them understand that there are two sides to every story, but to no avail.

Uncle Bill married three times; number two was Grace, who suffered mental illness. He was widowed again, but finally married Joan (I liked Joan). They lived originally in Deal, Kent, but moved to a very nice detached bungalow in Herne Bay. So at least Bill finally did himself proud from humble beginnings, as did two of my aunts; the eldest and the youngest. Florence (named after her mother) and Mary both married into good (and better off) families, and for that I'm very happy. Emma,

Beatrice and my mom lived similar lives to each other, but I'm certain they were just as happy, even if consigned to the cards that life had dealt them. Both Emma and Beatty had husbands, but for whatever reasons, I can't remember either of them having jobs. That's not to say they didn't, of course.

My mother's death in 1987 began the quick unravelling of a family (our immediate family) that had barely held together despite everything it had gone through since we were all children living under one roof with Mom, who somehow kept the "wolf from the door" and the authorities from taking us into care.

I remember one incident where Mom was on her hands and knees, scrubbing the living room floorboards with Dettol and water. The "housing woman", as we used to refer to the lady whose job it was, I suppose, to keep her eye on families like ours, didn't bother knocking before entering our house; instead, she just came through the hall and straight into the living room.

Mom looked up at her casually then continued scrubbing. The lady sighed, and said, 'Liza what are you doing, scrubbing floorboards? What's happened to the lino?'

'I've had to use it to keep the house warm for the kids,' Mom replied.

The housing woman told Mom that she shouldn't have to do this, and if she couldn't afford to keep the house warm in winter, 'Maybe you should think about having the children put into care for a while.'

‘Maybe if I didn’t keep the house clean and tidy and the kids as well, you might have a point. But the fact is, and you know this: both the house and my kids are as clean as a whistle. Now unless there’s anything else, you can be on your way.’

The lady wasn’t for turning. ‘Liza, you’re not listening. I’m trying to be of assistance here.’

‘I don’t need your assistance. I’ve had precious little of it so far, so off you go.’

The lady began to move forward towards Mom. Billy and I watched from the door that led to the stairs and our back door, which opened out to the toilet and coalhouse.

Our mother stood up, and hands on hips said, ‘If you don’t get out of this [not “my”] house, you see what’s in this bucket, I’ll tip the bloody lot over you.’ The lady then was for turning!

Mom was right. She did keep us as clean as she could, and did her housework religiously. It rubbed off on me, actually, because I’ve always kept my home in very clean and tidy order. Yes, we wore “hand me downs”, and the WVS helped us, but by and large, it was down to Mom and her determination to keep us all together. Sadly, however, as I said above, all those ties became loose, bedraggled and separated almost completely, after she died. These days, apart from most of my cousins, I have no relationship to speak of with any so-called “close” relatives outside my immediate family – I include my ex-wife Tina in my immediate family, my sons Marc and Tom, their partners Sarah and Laura, and my grandchildren.

Below is a poem I wrote ten years after my mother's passing:

***Christmas Past and Present***

*When I was a boy; I remember how times were very hard.*
*Mother did her best to feed us, on mainly bread and lard.*
*Christmastime was cosy, though most folk were poor,*
*Families were proud and hospitable; each house had an open door.*
*The Welfare man brought us toys, and Mother would wrap them all,*
*Dolls for the girls, perhaps a train for the boys, and*
*Home-made decorations and a Christmas tree, so tall.*
*Family ties meant everything as the years went rolling on,*
*We loved our mother and she loved us; ten years now she's been gone!*
*I miss her as much as I ever did, and no-one will ever know*
*How my heart yearns for those childhood days*
*And that Christmas of long ago.*
*The carol singers came to our door singing for free the yuletide verses*
*But sadly these days, if they don't get a quid, you only get threats and curses.*
*No festive spirit, and no goodwill, and nothing left to toast;*
*Scrooge is alive and kicking, in spite of Marley's ghost!*

# Chapter Eight

Bill Williams had worked really hard, as usual, to ensure that the two Camps of 1988 would have everything they needed, to continue the success his charity had thus far enjoyed. The shopping list was, I suppose, always difficult to write, with having to calculate how much of whatever was considered to be needed. John Preece had been cooking for most of the decade to date, so Bill left it to him, by and large

This is their list for both Camps, of meat to be ordered, and split into two collections; the first one being Thursday 28th July and the second on Thursday 11th August.

120lbs sausage (medium), 48lbs stewing beef (in 12lb bags), 48lbs mince (12lb bags), 4 shoulders pork (rolled and boned), spare ribs left in (cross cuts); 325 Burgers... and 650 fish fingers.

For the scheduled barbecue (first Camp): 50 Burgers, 50 sausage, 8 large breast of lamb, and 50 chicken portions. This was supplied by butcher Roy Coles.

The vegetables and other groceries, purchased from Passey & Jones, included: 1 crate cabbage, 1 case eggs, 1 sack onions.

Ken Spurling (former Camp staff) supplied the milk: 1 crate on first day, then as ordered.

I include these details because it is very interesting, I hope, to know what Camp meant in its various forms of continuation. The full list of boys from the West Midlands on the first Camp was:

**Wolverhampton:**

Christopher and Dennis Briody

Jason Carter x

Scott Darby

Shaun Brown x

Cagoo Bowen

Neil Mason

Delroy Morris

Keith Shingler

Darren, Neil and Gordon Taylor

John Wand

Wayne and Andrew Wright

Joshua Rafferty

**Sandwell:**

Harjit and Manjit Dhariwal

Scott Holmes x

Jamie Morris

Alan and Glen Newall

Michael Norman

Andrew Newhall

Darren and Kirk Saunders

James Thomas x

David Thomas x

Carl Walker

David Tromans x

**Walsall:**

Mark Chattaway

Christopher Halford

Christopher Harvey

Mark Hulley

Sean McLaughlin

Emerson and Martin Tolley

Dudley:

David and Louis Treasure

Callum Turner

'x' meant failed to arrive... apparently.

Also in 1988, the WRVS celebrated its Golden Jubilee

The Shropshire boys were:

David Price (Whitchurch)

Christopher Young (Shrewsbury)

G. Jones (Dawley

These are the younger boys (8 – 11 years old) from Shropshire who were members of our second Camp:

Oliver Young (Whitchurch)

Anthony Roe (Ludlow)

Michael Brooks (Whitchurch)

Dean Edwards (Shrewsbury)

Timothy Jones (Dawley)

Gareth and Christopher Price (Whitchurch)

I received the following letter from G. Jones (can't remember his Christian name). It is dated 8th November 1988:

*Dear Mr Scriven*

*I was wondering if you can call around to the above address I have a Xmas present for you. If you can will you please write a letter to tell me what day and time you are coming so I can be in on that day. The present is for letting me come to the Longmynd Adventure Camp for two weeks and I enjoyed myself at the Camp.*

*I was wondering if I can come back and I know we was the winning cabin in the competition and that was cabin two. It was myself and Neil Mason who kept writing the jokes on the paper, like (Good morning Bosun, we hope John is up to scratch) and other things like that.*

*At the moment I am off school with a bad cold. I hope this letter gets to you in time before you go to work driving the bus from Telford Town Centre to the Humbers and Muxton via Trench.*

*Got to close soon, see you soon when you come.*

*Yours sincerely*

*G. Jones*

*(Out of cabin two, that is Richard (George) and Wendy's (Smith) cabin).*

What a lovely letter. I can't remember actually going to pick up my present, but it was a very generous gesture, and typical of the kind of correspondence Bill had been receiving from lots of lads for decades. And now I was sharing the kindness. Proof if it were ever needed that the Camp was a resounding success story, year after year!

As I said above, the events which occurred between the latter part of the year and the spring of 1990 are covered in detail in my first book. As I've mentioned, the decision I made, which at the time I was utterly convinced was the right one, still haunts me to this very day! It haunts because of what (in my mind) resulted from it:

Bill refused to speak a single civil word to me for almost seven years.

The repercussions reverberated far and wide.

It undoubtedly gave a platform for the beginning of the end of our way of running the Camp, i.e. the committee gave itself a bigger say in how the Camp operated – remember that the overwhelming majority of members were clueless to the finer details of steering a ten-day Camp through its course. And Bill would never have allowed it to get that deeply involved in actual Camp business.

It was the underlying reason why I further infuriated the man I held the utmost respect for (writing a totally unnecessary scathing letter to Bill in 1996, albeit again thinking I was right at the time), which brought about my removal as Skipper by the committee, for that year's Camp). In fairness, I have to say that I wrote Barrie Gretton (Chair) a resignation letter (see below) on 25th May, after learning of my error in writing that damn letter to Bill. But when I informed them, individually, of Bill's acceptance of my apology (and requested they ignored my resignation letter), they stuck to their guns regarding replacing me. In fact, not one of them had the decency or courtesy to even reply to me.

*Dear Barrie*

*I feel totally ashamed of myself and deeply regret sending such a terrible letter to Bill, without first making enquiries as to his non-attendance at Pat Hazlehurst's funeral.*

*I am very sorry for bringing myself and my position of authority at Camp into disrepute; therefore I consider that I now have no alternative but to resign as Skipper.*

*I realise that perhaps you and possibly others may feel that this decision is unnecessary* but for myself (having behaved in such appalling fashion) and also for my peace of mind, I feel that resigning is in the best interests of everyone... and the continuation of the Camp.*

*I go however, feeling that the Camp is in good and sound order, and hoping it will continue to prosper. I feel very ashamed of myself to be honest; and that staying on after the way I have treated Bill, the one person in the whole world I wish I hadn't, is something I cannot consider. Bill was the nearest to a father I ever had, for all the time I knew him from being a boy on Camp through to that dreadful evening in 1989.*

*I feel sure that my replacement (Alan Preece) and his (Marc Scriven) will do a very acceptable job, and I strongly urge the committee to give them all the support and encouragement it can.*

*I would like to place on record my sincere thanks for all the support the committee has given me during the previous six years. I am totally gutted that I find myself feeling the need to resign so close to Camp '96, and that my long and successful (mostly) association with such a worthy cause, founded by Bill alone, should flounder in this awful manner!*

*I hate myself for what I've done, and for what I am doing now, to be perfectly honest.*

*I close offering yourself and our fellow committee members my sincere apologies for dragging you all into this horrible situation, by way of writing that garbage to Bill on official LAC paper.*

*Thank you for taking the time to read this letter Barrie.*

*Yours sincerely*

*Alan*

*p.s. I have written an unreserved apology to Bill.*

*They obviously didn't agree with that assumption because my apology to Bill brought not only acceptance, but his expressed wish for me to reconsider resigning. I did reconsider and as I said in book one, I wrote to every single member of the committee informing them of Bill's response... but received not one single reply! Maybe the wheels were set in slow motion for what happened in 1998?!

In contrast, though, how nice of Bill to say what he did. He was one special star in the whole of the galaxy, in my eyes. I deeply regret hurting him twice!

Back to 1990, and in truth the Camp was never the same again. Yes, we continued in the same format that Bill had operated under, in fact I knew no other way, and didn't want changes to the format, therefore none were made during my time at the helm, except for the odd tweak to the daily programme, perhaps. But it desperately needed Bill to return in order to have any hope of survival after our sponsors, the WRVS, decided in 1998 to change its policy regarding the support of children's holidays. What I'm saying is I think, nay know, Bill would have done more to save the Camp from dying by the hand of the WRVS Children's Holiday Chief Organiser (see book one) and the totally lethargic attitude of the committee.

Having had many years to ponder what went on back then, I can't help thinking that the committee's strategy might have been to accept every negative detail of my meeting with Hirst, in the hope that I would resign (because I was a definite thorn in their flesh), thus giving them carte blanche to run the Camp their way. Well, it has to at least be a possibility, all things considered.

I skippered the Camp up to and including 1997, and even though there had been a few problems, nothing prepared me for the fact that we would not be celebrating the Camp's Ruby (40$^{th}$) anniversary in1998!

# Chapter Nine

The new decade (1990) dawned with the release of Nelson Rolihlahla Mandela, after spending 27 years in a South African prison for his anti-apartheid views and committed stance against the country's regime.

The following year saw him inaugurated as the President of the African National Congress. And in 1994, the year after he was awarded the Nobel Peace Prize, Nelson Mandela became his country's president. Other titles bestowed upon him included the US Presidential Medal of Freedom, and the Soviet Order of Lenin. What a beautiful end to those years he spent incarcerated just for his political opinion.

Mr Mandela passed away on 5th December 2013, aged ninety-five years, some three weeks after our founder, Bill Williams BEM. Bill lived to reach eighty-seven years old.

On 25th April 1990, the space shuttle *Discovery* put the Hubble space telescope into orbit.

This was around the time that the LAC committee gave me a set of conditions to meet, in order for it to sanction my desire to skipper Camp 1990.

As the time for Camp loomed, I experienced feelings of trepidation.

I had satisfied the committee members, in the time between

Bill leaving and when I was offered the position, that I could skipper the Camp; they finally agreed (some four weeks before Camp was due to get underway) to give me a chance.

My sole reason for applying for the position of Skipper was to "steady the ship" until Bill's return. As I said in my first book, yes, I always wanted to be Skipper... but after Bill, not instead of him! I honestly thought that if I stood in, temporarily, for Bill ( instead of some "outsider") then the general format wouldn't alter.

Arriving at Camp on the morning of the first day, I hoped and prayed that all would go well. I also hoped and prayed that at some point during the ten days, Bill would show his face. Sadly, though, it was seven years before that prayer came to fruition... but my first one was answered in spades.

I decided to keep a logbook of sorts, to chronicle the day-to-day occurrences, and events of every Camp from then on. And on the inside cover of my journal, I wrote these words:

*The circumstances which have brought the Camp and me to this position are most unfortunate. Even now, I would hope that the situation can be sorted out. I would have preferred to become Skipper after Bill not instead of him.*

*Alan Scriven. July 1990.*

In no time at all, we were away! This was to be the forty-third Camp, in the charity's thirty-second year. And because the committee had decided on just one Camp per year, at least for the time being, the boys' ages ranged from eight to thirteen years. The potential problems of mixing the ages were discussed but I assured my fellow members, with the support of John Preece, that there was nothing to be concerned about. Bullying had never been an issue on any Camp, so why should this one be any different? My positive outlook and confidence proved correct.

I did, however, have to answer some awkward questions from the lads who had been to Camp on previous occasions, regarding why I was running this one. I simply told the lads that Skipper would be back (and I truly believed he would) but in the meantime I was in charge. The whole "company" accepted my response without further ado.

I mention in my first book my thoughts about remaining as Bosun instead of going straight to Skipper. My reasoning was because if Bill did return, or even visit us, there would be less confusion when he assumed (rightfully) his own title. I was dissuaded, however, by every person I put it to.

It proved to be a fantastic success, as 1979 had been, when I had last stood in the Skipper's shoes, albeit for a completely different reason!

The "Best Cabin" competition began in earnest, with Cabin Six opening up a one-point lead from One and Two. The eventual winners, Cabin Three, led by Andrew Wooldridge and Tony Hammond, didn't move into a leading position until the second

Saturday. Even after the Sports Day results had been added, Cabin Three only occupied third place. What won it for them was the Scavenger Hunt; a good result in a final (competitive) litter competition, and their Campfire performances.

So again, well done to Cabin Three members Mark Butterworth, Peter Rudd, Jason Millership, Melvin Winters, Tom Scriven, Justin Southam, Mathew O'Rourke and Michael Brookes, and of course their leaders (mentioned above).

The other lads on Camp 1990 were:

Cabin One: Leader Alan Preece. Russell Robinson, Gian Singh, Roy Pagett, Steven Lake, Tony Tinsley, Martin Wilkinson, Raymond Gale, Andrew Martin, Richard Lovatt.

Cabin Two: Leader Jon Harrison. Adrian Cottam, Paul Gallier, Graham Jones, Desroy Jones, Michael Jones, Peter James, Jason Harriman, James Davies.

Cabin Four: Leader John Trubshaw. David Cottam, Johnathan Cottam, Neil Platt, Simon Platt, Nicholas Platt, David Longston, Mark Hooks.

Cabin Five: Leader Neil Harrison. Gareth Price, Michael Anderson, Leslie Fullerton, David White, Jason Southam, Brian Gale, Adam Wardle.

Cabin Six: Leader Jim Hemsley. Michael Pargeter, Michael Hickman, Christopher Price, John Kearney (Best Camper), Chris Fellows, Frank Fellows, Gary Harris, Dean Hughes.

At this point, I would like to offer again, my sincere thanks to

John Trubshaw and the young ladies, Rachel, Jill, Julie and Sarah, who organised the overnight camping opportunities for the lads on this Camp.

Wendy Smith fulfilled the Bursar/Quarter Master position to a very high standard, which was nothing short of what I expected from her. An easily likeable northern lass, was Wendy, who took her turn in entertaining us in the staffroom with a few songs, including that very famous Yorkshire number: *On Ilkley Moor bar t'at*.

Over the years, our staffroom banter and sing-songs became almost the lifeblood of a happy Camp; if you could keep the staff happy, they performed their voluntary responsibilities over and above the required standard. During my time as both Bosun and Skipper, I gave the tent leaders (the hardest job of all) as much free time as I possibly could, and they appreciated it; rewarding Skipper and me with renewed commitment.

As I have said earlier, the Tent/Cabin competition was our only form of discipline. For that reason, we had to, er... tweak it a little bit, once or twice throughout the duration of a Camp, in order to maintain everyone's interest. No point (no pun intended) at all in trying to tell a group who are so far behind that they'll lose points for whatever misdemeanour that may have committed; they couldn't have cared less! So we had to keep a competitive spirit throughout, or at least until the final few days, because that way the group that wins has, over the ten days of Camp, deserved it. Bill taught me the art of "tweaking" the points system during my time as Bosun.

Looking at the table for 1990, I revisited the various reasons given as to why points were awarded. These included Cabin Inspections (as always); Tables (first to finish their washing up); Litter Picks; Football Competition; Volunteers; Sports Day results; Good behaviour; Games, including Harbour Light. This is a night game, the details of which are included in my previous books, and one the vast majority of children absolutely loved.

It was very rare for points to be deducted.

In 1983, we celebrated the Camp's Silver Jubilee, and as a lasting memory of this historical event, Skipper Williams commissioned a number of Dunoon Pottery mugs, and t-shirts, to commemorate this brilliant milestone. Each child was given one of each, and the staff received a sweatshirt in either red, like the t-shirts, or blue. The left-over items were stored away until 1990, when I decided to use them as prizes at the Campfire. And it surprised me somewhat to see the response of the children who received a memento of that historic year... they loved them!

Expenses for 1990 included: MEB fridge freezer £150, T. Beaman (committee member) plumbing work £52:98, empty cesspool £97:50, Calor Gas £13.64, Skip Hire £54.05, Clee Hill Chest Freezer £240, and the actual ten-day Camp cost: £1,215.76.

At the committee's Annual General Meeting held on 1st Feb 1991, the members confirmed that they were happy and satisfied with the job I had done, with the help of my staff, of course, the majority of whom were "old hands" who had remained loyal to the Camp if not me, and for that alone, I remain very grateful.

The meeting was marred, however, by Francis Rudge's insistence that I hand over the key to the Skipper's caravan to him. I absolutely refused, on the grounds that any letting of the Camp (which at the time he was responsible for) did not include the caravan, which had been given to the Camp; not me, him, Bill, or anyone else! That might sound like a contradiction, but the fact was that the caravan was never included in the letting of the site and its facilities. And back in 1986 (if memory serves), it was agreed that the caravan should be used as the Skipper's "headquarters", so no part of the fixtures included in the letting of the premises.

This veiled demand by Francis, and my "stubbornness" came to a dramatic climax when a vote on whether or not I should succumb was motioned. The vote resulted in an equal number, for and against. Barrie Gretton, the chair of the committee, had the casting vote. He used it to the advantage and delight of Mr Rudge, but still I refused to hand over the only key to the caravan, until I was advised to do so by a very dear friend, whom ironically, had proposed it at the said meeting...

On 9th April 1991, I received the following letter from fellow committee member, and former West Mercia Police Superintendent Pat Hazlehurst QPM.

*Dear Alan*

*I was so pleased on Thursday when you said, finally, that you would give up that blasted key; although you have consistently argued against a previous democratic committee decision!*

*I know, however, that you will not break your word to me, we have been friends for a very long time <u>so be a dear and put the damn thing in an envelope and send it to me.</u>*

*I can then say 'Alan has found the key', and that will knock the wind out of their sails. Remember, there's more ways of killing a cat than wringing its neck.*

*What we all have to bear in mind is that each one of us must at times, forget our own personal feelings, and remember that it is the children who matter. Every bit of our energy must be concentrated on that fact. Each of us must utilise our individual qualities to that end.*

*You, Alan, have superb qualities for understanding and handling those children, and we all know that there are those amongst us who cannot do that.*

*When I was younger and fitter I did what I could in the kitchen to keep people fed. I am so pleased that John is doing such a good job at Camp now. I won't be as useless as I was in 1990, God willing; I'll bake a few cakes this year.*

*Peter and Barrie have business expertise which they use for the benefit of the Camp. None of us have that, or their contacts, so their contribution is vital.*

*Francis living so near to the Camp, and with all the time in the world, is obviously the one to see to the letting of it etc. Let us not begrudge him the satisfaction he gets from doing this.*

*If you show that you are above petty squabbling you emerge the winner. You have the intelligence Alan, so should have no difficulty in doing this.*

*Now send me the key.*

*Yours as ever*

*Pat x*

The many letters I received from Pat over a period of some twenty-eight years are a very valued possession. I will include at least one more before the end of this book. She was as straight as a dye, was Pat, and a very good friend to Bill as well as to me. Indeed, Pat and Bill went back a long way, and were former colleagues.

For the 1991 Camp, I promoted my friend Alan Preece to the role of Bosun. I had given that coveted position to my brother David for my first Camp as Skipper (proper), but he failed miserably. His future help was confined to the kitchen, which if he's honest, he enjoyed far more than his field responsibilities. He loved working with John Preece.

David was, however, one of the best tent leaders I ever worked with throughout my time with the Camp; Dean

Nightingale was the other 'stand-out' member of staff.

David and Dean were also extremely useful in the kitchen. The policy (with one exception: yours truly) had always been that anyone who joined the staff immediately following their time as a beneficiary went into the kitchen, at least for one Camp. This was never a problem with whoever was doing the cooking, but if (and it did happen) the cook's opinion was that the youngster wasn't up to scratch, then he would be assigned to one of the more experienced tent leaders, in an attempt to discover whether his talents lay on the field side of the staff. Sadly, however, the record books aren't bursting with names of former Campers who became successful tent leaders.

Alan was a very experienced tent leader, and could turn his hand to most things, which was an obvious bonus after Francis decided to quit (as described in my first book).

I just thought he might be better in the Bosun's position than David. My judgement was correct, I feel, so no hard feelings, I hope, from my erstwhile brother...

Cabin Six, under the leadership of our newest tent leader, Nicola Piggott, won the Cabin competition, so congratulations to Simon Pippard, Mathew Pippard, Shamil Lal, Stuart Robertson, Stephen Dulson, Mathew Gordon, Craig Clarke... and of course Nicky.

We gave a total of forty-nine lads a holiday in 1991, and every one of them had a fantastic time! Brothers usually chose to be in the same tent, but that wasn't the case with Shamil and

Sanjeer Lal, because Sanjeer opted to join the ranks of Cabin One. There were six sets of brothers on Camp 1991; we always gave brothers the option of staying together or splitting. The rule was, though, that whichever way you went (my brothers and I always stayed together), you stuck it out. This condition was broken once or twice in exceptional circumstances, but as a rule... no.

The full list of boys (and tent leaders) on our 1991 Camp (as well as Cabin 6) was as follows:

Cabin One: Leaders Marc Scriven and Mark Steadman. Marcus Cohen, Sanjeer Lal, Robert Burns, Isaac Henry, John Kearney, Lee Johnson, Adam Danks, Stephen Galea.

Cabin Two: Leader Jon Harrison. Frank Fellows, Chris Fellows, Brian Fullerton, Leslie Fullerton, Ashley Timmins, Scott Murphy, Lee Avey, Thomas Scriven (my son), Andrew O'Brien.

Cabin Three: Leaders Jim Hemsley and Andrew Wooldridge. Brian Hurdman, Gary Harris, Mathew Hodgkinson, Mark Hodgkinson, James Mohammed, Keith Grainger, Gavin Hyde, Dean Hughes.

Cabin Four: Leader Andrew Butler. David Cosgrove, Peter Coney, Nicholas Williams, Simon Williams, Sean Williams, Richard Hurdman, Michael Pargeter, Daniel O'Brien.

Cabin Five: Leaders Tony Hammond and Jeremy Kenny. Neil Gilbert, Ashley Bevan, John Lenton, David Hall, David Gillespie (Best Camper), Michael Brookes, Neil Bloomfield, Daniel Young.

On this Camp, I was very glad of the occasional help from Richard George, and Jim Bremner. Richard (an “old hand”) would have been a first-choice tent leader, if he could have been with us for the duration. Jim very kindly provided our lads with some outdoor pursuits, which included rock climbing and canoeing. Jim was a former “Special Forces” soldier, who owned and ran a leisure activities company. He and I became good friends, and I was very saddened to hear of his passing in 2018. God bless you, Jimmy.

As in 1990, John Trubshaw and his daughter Laura supervised the overnight camping at Brow Farm.

I felt I was settling into the job of “minding the shop” until Bill returned.

But our “blessed” Camps came to a sudden and unexpected harsh bump in 1992!

Again, the details are well documented in my first book, so all I’ll say here is... well, it was a mighty and very trying struggle; bloody hard work to say the very least, and the closest we ever came to ending a Camp prematurely, by sending the lads home. For those of you not familiar with our problems in 1992, a nasty and aggressive stomach bug invaded our peace, and it caused havoc! It was “only” a twenty-four-hour bug, the local doctor told us, but it lasted almost the entire duration of that particular holiday, with lads and staff (myself included) catching the bug as the days rolled on. We seriously considered closing the Camp down early, but the doctor's advice was not to, because we had it contained.

I would like to pay tribute now to all the souls that were with me on that dreadful ride (all named below), and to offer again, my sincere gratitude to each and every one of them.

Staff: Alan Preece (Bosun), Wendy Smith (Bursar/QM), David Scriven (Ass't QM), John Preece (Cook)*, Dean Nightingale (Kitchen), Marc Scriven (Kitchen), Patrick Harte (Kitchen).
Tent Leaders on Camp 1992: Jim Hemsley, Phil Woods (C1); Vinnie Price, Andrew Butler (C2); Steff Latewood (C3); Andy Dawson, Jon Harrison, Gordon Harris (C4); Tony Hammond, Peter Jukes (C5); Nicola Piggott, Mark Butler (C6)

Some cabins, in fact all of them, save Cabin Three, had more than one leader. This was due either to the fact that some leaders would have to leave early, or one of them were young or inexperienced... or both! It was a time-honoured policy (numbers of staff allowing) not to overload new members of the field staff.

The Children:
Cabin One: Mark Mellor, Shane Bentley, Calvin Bailey, Mathew Tillett, David Sutton, Robert Foxall, Ian Burton, Craig Burton, Sidney Stevens.

Cabin Two: Mark Cooke, Dale Powell, Jed Powell, Carl Pritchard, Adam Payne, Michael Stone, Steven Smith, James Smith, Peter Coney.
Cabin Three: Wayne Hyde, Shaun Hyde, Lee Cattell, Ashley Timmins, Keith Grainger, Mathew Ball, Marcus Chambers, Barry Burton.
Cabin Four: John Lenton, Mark Lenton, Barry Nicholas, Philip Nicholas, David Davies, David Timmins, Mark Lycett, Michael Lycett, David Cannon.
Cabin Five: Gavin Jones, Gavin Lee Bentley, Carl Clutton, Craig Clutton, Mathew Jones, Gareth Hughes, Paul Hughes, James Tillett.
Cabin Six: Wayne Timmins, Neil Timmins, Frank Fellows, Tom Scriven, Brian Fullerton, Leslie Fullerton, Michael Malpass, Mark Stevens, Jamie Preece.

I received this letter (dated 20/08/92) from Pat Hazlehurst, shortly after that dreadful Camp had been assigned to history. I had asked her to write the "thank you" letters for me:

*Dear Alan*
*As I said at the committee meeting on Sunday - you missed one name off the list of those to be thanked, and that was* *__yours!__*
*I've known you a long time, Alan; my first positive memory was of you presenting a pipe and tobacco to Bill, probably twenty-five years ago.*

*That impressed me so much, and you have done a lot more since, which backed up my thought then, which was "this kid is a giver not a taker".*

*And when were you called upon to give, and endure more than on this last Camp? I am not surprised that you went home and collapsed for three days; I was worried about you, and the very look of you at Campfire.*

*You suffered as others did, and how you kept going, I'll never know, but we are all grateful for that.*

*At least I feel some good will come out of it all, and if we can get the "plumbing" fixed, life will be a lot easier.*

*Not least of what we and the children have to be thankful for is the way you took over (even if with some hesitation) and ran the Camp when Bill finished.*

*You have been more than a worthy successor to him.*

*With my love and gratitude always*

*Pat.*

Pat's final two sentences in her letter are by no means a slight on Bill. They were the very best of friends, and work colleagues, Pat was simply being nice to me after the nightmare of Camp 1992.

*Skipper Bill Williams with some of the boys, in Minton Batch, early 1960s*

*Mrs Robin Hazlerigg (WVS Chief Childrens Holiday Organiser during the Camp's early years).*
*Don Mansell (tent leader 1960s is behind her)*

*The very first group (1959), and the very last group (1997)*

*Me overseeing a sports day event (1980s)*

*Owen Lewis's group 1980s*

*Former Campers Ian "Scottie" Gibbons, Charles Gunter and me, with former tent leader Mick Powell*

*Unveiling of the Bill Williams memorial bench summer 2019. Bill's daughters Ann (L) and Debbie seated. Former Bishop (and Camp volunteer 1960s) Richard Lewis (centre) in blue shirt*

# Chapter Ten

I felt that for the 1993 Camp it might be a lot better, easier, and healthier for everyone, especially the children (our top priority always) and their leaders, if we went back to proper Camping in canvas ridge tents. I put this to my Bosun, Alan Preece. His welcome response was that I had "pinched the thought right out of his head". So it was decided, at least between the two of us. There was the formality of advising the committee (of which I had been a member since 1981), but I considered it just that: a formality.

Bill had always insisted that the committee had no sway over the actual Camps. It was, he repeated many times, originally created to acquire charity status, raise funds, and to ensure the continuity of that necessary deed. Naturally, I concede, it got a lot more involved following Bill's untimely "retirement" from the charity (details of how this affected the actual Camps are explained in my first book), so I felt I had to discuss it at the next meeting, after Alan and I had decided on the path we were taking. The first person we spoke to was John Preece as he was, like me, a committee member. He agreed, so I knew I had at least one on board. The outcome, in fact, was total agreement with our decision, and the cabins would be used for spare staff (not including tent leaders) accommodation, and storage, which was always in short supply.

Alan Preece sourced the tents from the army, thus allowing us to get back to basics, so to speak. On setting-up day, the weather was atrocious; indeed, it had rained almost non-stop all night, and because of the building of the new toilet/shower block, after the previous year's chaos, the back field was in no fit state to pitch tents on. Actually, it wouldn't be over-exaggerating to say that we couldn't have used the cabins to house the children anyway, so the tents became an absolute necessity.

Alan and I decided therefore that the tents would have to be pitched on the front field. This practice obviously narrowed down our onsite games space; we managed, however, as we always did. As well, we had the opportunity to make even more use of Minton Batch.

I knew that there was a possibility of a "wind change" in the air, regarding the future of the Camp, due to apparent policy changes of our sponsors, the WRVS. The details (once again) are mentioned in my first book. But I just continued on, perhaps burying my head in the sand, I suppose, in a vain attempt to shut out the impending storm clouds.

I refused to let my mind wander to what might happen in the future, except as always to hope that Bill Williams, the true Skipper, would show up and save the Camp from any hostility the "jungle drums" might be foretelling!

I was still very upset about what had happened three years earlier. I thought the absolute world of Bill; he had been to me the father I always wanted, and it's difficult even now, three decades later, to think of the whole mess of Bill's exit without shedding a tear!

It's hard to put it into words, to be honest. I loved him; I suppose we all did. I am in no way trying to suggest that I had the monopoly of his attention; indeed, the hundreds of letters back and forth between him and many of the lads over his thirty-two years with the Camp bear testimony to that. But to me, when I was a child, he was the most important person in my life, next to my mom. And then as I matured into a young man, proving myself as a tent leader, my admiration of him just went through the roof!

There were other people (famous) whom I admired as I grew up: George Best; Joan Baez; Elvis, of course... and the Beatles, to name just a few. But Bill was doubly special. And I'm sure 99.9% of the people whose lives he touched felt exactly the same. The hardest period of my life was the years when Bill absolutely refused to speak to me. I only saw him once during that now far-off "cold war" between us; it was at the annual West Midlands Show in Shrewsbury. Our eyes locked for the briefest moment before he walked off. I thought it would be pointless to go after him, so I turned and walked away. The hurt was indescribable; as no doubt Bill's was after he said I had betrayed him.

The point I wish to make is that when I contacted his eldest daughter Annie about the possibility of my first book being published, she very kindly agreed to meet me. I was dreading it, for obvious reasons.

After lunching together in Shrewsbury, during which time I had tried to explain my side of our (mine and her dad's) fall-out, I gave Annie a raw copy of my book to read through, promising that anything she wasn't happy with, I would exclude.

After a few days, we spoke again. I nervously waited for Annie's opinion. I need not have worried. She very graciously told me she was happy with it, and that I should go ahead. I had been worried mostly, and obviously, about what she thought about what had happened to cause her dad's departure from the Camp. And also the fact that it was all in the book... because I wanted to write a true and concise account, including all the politics of the first forty years of the charity's history.

Annie's words were: "If it happened, then include it."

When my book was published, I gave Annie and her younger sister Debbie a copy. And after reading it, they both paid me the magnanimous compliment of saying that they had gained a brother. Thank you, ladies, very much. It meant everything to me to know that Bill's daughters hadn't wanted to judge me.

In early April 1993, I was given a copy of a written record of Pat Hazlehurst's "interview" by a few members of the WRVS, in particular the actual interviewer, Elsa Loxton. The others present were Mrs Margaret Saint, Mrs Jess Buttery and Mrs Joan Whitley. The recorder was Mr George Glover.

The purpose of the interview was, apparently to "discuss some aspects of the work done by the WRVS from the end of the war". Pat was invited to answer questions about her experience with the Longmynd Adventure Camp.

I make no apology for regularly featuring "Pat H", as we used to refer to her, because I very much doubt that I am the only one who considers that she was second only to Bill in the Camp's "hierarchy". Pat was there for Bill from almost the very beginning, and was still involved right up to her death at eighty-three years old, in April 1996:

***Elsa:*** *I am Elsa Loxton, and if you go back to the WRVS records you will find me as Elsa Allen-Jones. We are going to discuss some aspects of [the work] WRVS was asked to do, we were trained to say yes; we said no to nobody. Consequently, the range of our work is quite enormous.*

*It's a job to know where to start. I think possibly, we will start with the work we did for children, which involved helping with the distribution of orange juice and cod liver oil for clinics. From that, grew the welfare of the children in the county council homes. I think probably the best person we could get to talk about this would be Pat Hazlehurst, because Pat has been involved with work for children for a great many years, and knew the people who worked for the children on behalf of the WRVS for a very long time.*

*What are your recollections, Pat?*

***Pat H:*** *Firstly, I am not a member of the WRVS but I did know Robin Hazlerigg very well indeed; we used to get mixed up, my name being Hazlehurst. She was concerned, when I first knew her, with a Camp that had been running near Minton in South Shropshire. The Camp was brought about by a scheme which gave holidays to deprived children. Others were housed in the Shropshire area for anything up to a fortnight.*

*There were two Camps for a time; one for boys, and one for girls. I was involved with the boys Camp, and I would like people to be aware that because of the valuable work done by the WRVS in those early days, this Camp, the boys', is still going strong, and I remain very much committed to it.*

*What I think is so pleasing is that not only over the years have I seen the operating so successfully, but also, I am now seeing some of the boys I remember as 12-year-olds, who are now grown men and are responsible for the day to day running of the Camp.*

*The Camp is now much more sophisticated compared to the early years. The man who started it all was a Shropshire police officer called Bill Williams, who was awarded the British Empire Medal in 1983 for all his hard work and effort to get the Camp up and running on a permanent basis. From the early sixties, the Camp was situated in the most unholy position, really. The field sloped, but the top part, where the tents were pitched, was relatively flat.*

*Thanks to the good work of Robin Hazlerigg, and some help from her late husband's estate, we managed to get a concrete double garage built on the field. We used half of it as the kitchen, because up till then all the cooking was done in one end of a big marquee which we hired for the duration of the Camps, two per year at that time; the children ate their meals in there, too. I think the other half was used as a staffroom facility.*

*The boys slept in tents. The toilets were portable Elsanols, and a trough for the obvious, screened off with old sacks; very basic indeed, but they loved it, and still do, although we have made decent progress since those days when the lad running it now was a boy on Camp himself. He found himself too old to be at Camp in the late sixties, but Bill kept him on as a junior member of staff, and he has returned every year since making his way through "the ranks" as he did so. I'm very proud of him.*

*The lads washed in the brook that ran through the bottom of the field; they'd try every trick in the book, some of them, to avoid this, and who could blame them (laughs); I wouldn't have fancied it.*

*The cooking was done brilliantly by a lovely old WVS lady from the Black Country, who spoke very much the same language as the boys, although she originated from up north.*

*I have always supported the Camp, and attended every*

*Campfire. I retired from the force in 1973, as did Bill, for health reasons, unfortunately. The lady that cooked, Mrs Hull, had a serious accident which ended her involvement with the Camp. This caused a big problem for Bill. He kept telling me how much he needed a cook, and looking at me in that way, you know, the look that's saying, will you do it please.*

*Elsa said earlier that you learn never to say no; well believe me, you couldn't say no to Bill Williams. If he needed money, he got it. If he required a service, he got it. So I agreed to cook for him on Camp. Well now, the most I had ever cooked for was perhaps a dozen, at a stretch. But I found myself in this primitive kitchen with a Calor gas stove, which was obsolete by the way; no hot water; no running water even. It had to be fetched in a tanker from Minton.*

***Joan:** Had you ever been a girl guide, Pat?*

***Pat H:** Well yes, although I never got my arm full of badges. It was the spirit of the Camp which made it all so wonderful. I can't actually put it into words you'd understand, if you don't mind me saying, what a fantastic place the Camp has always been. Once one has experienced the magical aura of the place, you never want to leave.*

*We had a forester who lived near the Camp, and he, like Bill, knew absolutely everyone. If we had a problem, like for instance the gas ran out whilst I was cooking breakfast one*

*Sunday morning, Francis would say "leave it to me", and he'd be off. Half an hour later he'd be back with a bottle of gas he had borrowed from a local farmer. This is how we worked; how we got on and sorted stuff under very primitive conditions. We struggled and we strove to succeed. And we did succeed!*

***Elsa:*** *But it was the spirit that we had experienced during the war years that kept us going, wasn't it?*

***Pat H:*** *It was, and the point was that throughout all those times, difficult or otherwise, at Camp, you would look up and see Robin Hazlerigg standing there. And she didn't come over as the gracious lady to patronise the kids; no, she came into the kitchen and said to the cook, whether it was me or another, "What can I do to help?" I tell you now that if I had said that the kitchen floor needed scrubbing, she would have done it without question. But we had people for that sort of thing, let me tell you; I never scrubbed the floor!*

*But what has struck me over the years I have been involved with the Camp, and I'm still involved today, is that it was started by the WVS; it was involved from the minute Bill Williams had the idea to give some deprived lads from the West Midlands a country holiday. No one connected to the Camp is in any doubt of the sterling work that the WRVS (now) continues to do to help make it continually succeed.*

*Another brilliant success story is the fact that the Camp is now run by men who were former boys on the Camp back in the sixties; indeed, the chap who now has overall responsibility for the Camp, and the lads has been a permanent fixture since I think, 1965; what an amazing achievement. And obviously, I am very proud to call these men my friends.*

*We have committee meetings; I am the secretary. And occasionally they are held at my house. Well, a couple of years ago I was ill whilst the Camp was in operation, so couldn't attend any of the special days like Sports Day or Campfire night, and worst of all, I couldn't go along and help them, as I have always done. Well, on the final Sunday, in the afternoon, these three lads came to visit me, bearing chocolates and flowers. The boys of the Camp, who have won an award during the ten days, are presented with a certificate. Well, lo and behold, Alan, the Skipper, presented me with a certificate, honouring my years of service to The Longmynd Adventure Camp. I began to weep with happiness and pride; John, the cook said, "I'd better make you a pot of tea then Pat, that'll sort you out."*

*That's the spirit of the Camp which we mentioned earlier, Elsa. And that was inspired in no small part, by the WRVS, and in particular, Robin.*

***Elsa:** Pat, before we finish talking about the children, I think it's important to mention too, that a good number of children from the Black Country not only went to Pat's Camp in Stretton;*

*some went into private homes in Shropshire didn't they, particularly countryside homes. They had to unlearn a lot of strange urban habits, I think, but got to enjoy the homes.*

***Pat H:*** *Maybe the ones who went to those homes, perhaps. But Bill Williams' philosophy was, for Camp anyway, we are here to give these lads a holiday, not to change or reform them. Unfortunately, Bill is no longer connected with the Camp, but his influence goes on, through Alan. He operates in exactly the same successful way that Bill did.*

*Admittedly, my vocabulary was enriched by what I heard from some of those children; but the quality always shone through; honest and genuine kids. We get what's called a case history on each child, so Bill knew what problems or difficulties he might have to deal with. But do you know, he hardly ever had to even look at them. And it's just the same with Alan.*

*The Camp is doing a tremendous amount of good for the socially deprived child, as it has since its inception, and long may it continue to do so.*

***Elsa:*** *On behalf of us all, Pat, thank you very much indeed for coming to talk to us about the Camp, and the children.*

The "case history" offered very little information about the child – I would love to have seen mine, though – hence, I suppose, the reason we didn't study them.

During my years as Skipper, I can honestly say that only on two occasions did I have cause to consult case history forms. When I was Bosun, under Bill, he informed me of their existence; showing me one, and saying that if I thought that looking at them (or whoever it was that might perhaps have reason to look) would help, then I was free to do so. But generally, they remained in their envelope untouched.

I have to say however, that some children, over the years, did come from less than what could be called acceptable circumstances, if their stories were to be believed. Usually, however, and especially with the Shropshire lads, the social worker or the WRVS ladies, Kim Harris of Shrewsbury in particular, would advise us of anything we ought to know about the youngsters she brought to Camp. I don't intend to mention any names because that would not be fair to the child, but sometimes we did wonder what we might be sending them back to if the lads' descriptions of "home life" were accurate; which to be honest, was hardly ever the case. Sadly, however, people's perceptions were harder to change.

But as Pat H says, we were only there to give them a holiday they wouldn't otherwise have, and that's exactly what we did... in spades!

The total personnel on Camp 1993:

Staff: Alan Scriven (Skipper), Alan Preece (Bosun), Wendy Smith (QM), John Preece (Cook), Dean Nightingale, David Scriven

(Kitchen), Tony Hammond, Annie Williams, Kevin Duggins (Part-time help).

In the Tents:

Tent One: Leader Steff Latewood. Christopher Hewlett, Richard Wallsworth, Michael Williams, Jason Phillips, Michael Winters, Nigel Phillips, Shaun Hyde, Wayne James, Kevin Moss.

Tent Two: Leader Marc Scriven; Stephen Phillips (Ass't). John Locke, Stephen Johnson, Lee Johnson, David Cameron, Stuart Parkes, Mark Shenton, Jason Smith, Jamie Preece, Philip Busby*.

Tent Three: Leader Phil Woods. Mathew Lockley, Mark Perry, Thomas Scriven, Carl Selby, Wayne Hyde, Lee Sutton, Alan Sutton, Brian Handley, Michael Myles.

Tent Four: Leader Nicky Piggott; Michael Pargeter (Ass't). Richard Wellsbury*, James Hardwick, Mathew Hewlett, Richard Pargeter, Mark Goode, John Richards, David Richards, Daryl Harris, Johnathan Gibbon, Jamie Malpass.

Tent Five: Leader Andrew Dawson. Zenon Wozniak, David Hewlett, Andrew Locke, Richard Mold, David James, Philip Ball, Duane Ball, Gareth Lyons, Michael Lyons.

Tent Six: Leader Kevin Smith. Frank Fellows, Lester Plant, Steven Mold, James Jones, Simon Platt, Paul Dulson, Paul Southey, Nicholas Platt, David Readman.

This year, it was the turn of Tent Five to win the coveted tent marks competition.

*My records show me that Richard and Philip swapped tents on the third day. This was a most unusual practice. The reason for the swap is not documented, however, and that was a most unusual practice, too!

Skipper Williams would never have allowed such a thing to happen. You picked your tent (he and I always tried to accommodate individual preferences), and you stuck with it. So for me to actually allow the swap, it must have been a good reason. Neither of them had a brother in the tent they moved into, so I can't put my finger on it... strange, that!

Two medical situations arose on this Camp, which caused me to consult the so called case history of each child involved.

One had to be taken to Church Stretton Dentist. Here is the report I sent to the relevant authorities:

*XX had been suffering distress for the previous 3 / 4 days, owing to a very painful tooth.*

*Having arranged an emergency appointment at Church Stretton Dentists, we took him along this morning at 09:30hrs.*

*I took XX's "case history" and consent forms with me. It was decided by Mr Lyness after examination, to extract the offending tooth. XX's mouth was frozen for the procedure, which was successful. XX then returned to Camp with no further problems.*

*He is resting at present, and is very happy and comfortable.*

The second case was an entirely different scenario:

*XX has said he is suffering from asthma, and has (he said) had a number of "attacks". It is the opinion of trained medics working on the Camp, however, that he is not.*

*He says he is using his father's inhaler. I find this rather disturbing, considering the possible effects this could have on the child if this disclosure is fact!*

*His WRVS report (case history) offers no mention whatsoever of this, or any alleged illness.*

*I have to say that most of the time the lad is fine and no trouble at all. At the beginning of Camp however, he complained of pains, as did his younger brother.*

*I am inclined to conclude that this was a "sympathy seeking" tactic, especially as it happened during a visit by Mrs Roscoe (WRV).*

*A Scriven; LAC Leader, 1993*

Both lads were given a clean bill of health.

A nice picture of me, with Michael Williams and Richard Mold, appeared in the *Shropshire Star* newspaper during Camp '93.

# Chapter Eleven

An interesting article, written by Alfred Bee, appeared in a local Church Stretton "giveaway" magazine in 1993 (post-Camp). I thought it might give the reader another independent view of the Camp. It was written under the heading *Clubs and Societies* and accompanied by a photograph of the main building.

*For two weeks every August, the Stretton Hills near Minton echo to the shouts and laughter of about fifty boys, aged between 8 and 13, who have come from various parts of Shropshire and the Midlands inner cities to enjoy a holiday at the Longmynd Adventure Camp.*

*It all began thirty-five years ago when Bill Williams, then the local policeman in Wistanstow, organised a Camp for some less fortunate children. It was a great success, and later the Camp was formally established as a registered charity with the aim of providing country holidays for "socially deprived" children.*

*Selection of the children is made by Social Services [and the WRVS] on the grounds of need. Sometimes the children need a break from uncaring or violent parents, or perhaps the parents just cannot afford to give their children a holiday.*

*The Camp staff are all willing volunteers; most - including Alan Scriven, the "Skipper" - being themselves "ex kids" who give up two weeks of their time every year to return the favour, and give a little happiness and excitement to these children, whose lives probably lack the loving and caring relationships that most of us take for granted.*

*The Camp aims to provide an atmosphere of comradeship and friendship in a disciplined environment with inter-tent sports and competitions being organised, and extra points being awarded for good manners and behaviour! Team spirit quickly develops in the heat of friendly rivalry, and for many of the children this will be the first opportunity for them to form such bonds. A cross country race to the top of the Ragleth Hill tests their stamina, and gives them an opportunity to see our glorious views at first hand.*

*Other walks and visits help them to see the better side of life. Hopefully experience of the Camp will assist in improving their characters, and play a real part in encouraging them to be good citizens.*

*The continuing success of the Camp has been due, in no small measure to the support, both financial and practical, of individuals and organisations in our local community: indeed, it could not survive without such help, as each Camp costs in the region of £2,000 to run. Many years ago, Rotary Club helped build the original toilet block, whilst Round Table financed the drilling for the Camp's own water supply, and physically dug the trenches for the water pipes! Both organisations have continued their association with the Camp; Roy Field's magic show being an annual highlight. And trips to Mr and Mrs Lloyd's swimming pool at All Stretton are a long-standing fixture. Plus, this year, for the very first time, the superb facilities at Manor Adventure Camp were made available for three days.*

*Feeding the children is a mammoth exercise in itself. They get three full meals a day, with not a chip insight! Local ladies bake cakes (imagine how many cakes 55 hungry boys and 16 staff can get through in ten days); traders donate surplus food stocks, and this year a tin collection point was set up in Saverite by Ladies Group, who also sponsored a trip to the seaside. It is hardly believable that for some of the children, this was their first sight of the sea, other than on television.*

*A new toilet and shower block has recently been built at a cost of over £20,000, and it is hoped that the kitchen facilities will be renovated in the near future, if funds permit.*

*The Camp committee, under the chairmanship of Mr Barrie Gretton, is hoping that in the near future it will be possible to organise two Camps per year* [as was the "norm" up until Bill left] *and also to increase the letting of the site to other youth-orientated organisations, and Social Service groups. A party of disabled children recently spent a most enjoyable week there.*

*The support of the people of the Strettons for this annual Camp is greatly appreciated by the Committee, and the fact that some of the under-privileged lads have now grown up and returned to help staff the Camp redounds to the credit of the local community, and to those who give their time and talents to this worthwhile venture.*

*The committee would be very happy for people to see the Camp in operation; in particular, there is a warm invitation to anyone who would like to attend the Open Night, and barbecue on the evening before the Camp starts.*

Not a bad article, all things considered, but I would beg to disagree with his suggestion that there was a lack of love and caring in the boys' home lives. From my experience, both from my own childhood, and that of most of the lads who came to Camp, this assumption has no grounds whatsoever! We were poor, extremely so, the great majority of us. But we were loved! Indeed, as I mention in my first book, my mother loved all her children unconditionally, and as much as two parents could have. As for violence in the home; if any of this went on, I never knew of it.

Mr Bee isn't alone in his thinking; I've encountered such assumptions on many occasions. It seems to be a given: if you are selected for a holiday with the Longmynd Adventure Camp, then no one loves you, or cares for you; and your parents behave violently towards you.

Wrong... in the majority of cases, in my opinion.

Another error in Mr Bee's article involves the Ladies Group of Church Stretton. They, as far as I am aware (and I think I would know) never sponsored any of our trips to the seaside. They may have made a donation which was put towards the cost of the trip, but the sponsorship came courtesy of the WRVS. It gave a moderate sum of money for each child's place (this was because, in the words of Bill Williams BEM, "we don't want to kill the goose that lays the golden egg"); any and all donations on top of this went towards ensuring that the children were given a holiday they would remember, hopefully, for a very long time... a lifetime, some of us!

Camp 1994 got off to a bad start, politically; this is explained in detail in my first book. It also covers the row I had with my cook (and close friend) John Preece, which resulted in me not asking John for his help on any future Camps.

It was a strange Camp when I look back: changes to staff positions (massive mistake); a child's self-inflicted injury (which threatened to put me in the dock on a charge of neglect - thankfully this was shown not to be the case); children taken home (unsuitable for Camp, or Camp was unsuitable for them); no visitors to Campfire, with the exception of three committee colleagues; two brothers going AWOL; the general behaviour of the lads was appalling; terrible weather (forcing the cancellation of the Ghost Hunt for the first time in the Camp's history); wives/girlfriends of staff turning up (inevitably distracting the staff, which the lads took full advantage of); an electrical storm in the early hours (that was a sight to behold), and an indoor "Campfire" (I felt I couldn't trust the lads to behave around a real bonfire).

This Camp, for the reasons above (and more) proved to be the worst one I was ever involved with, including 1992. There are more details of Camp '94 in book one.

I have to say, however, that this Camp was the exception to the rule, in many ways. Most notably, the extremely poor behaviour of the majority. The continued bad behaviour was regularly off the scale; obviously there was, and always would be, maybe one or two who would do their best to cause a bit of upheaval; these, though, were usually straightened out by their peers. The lad who I took home was one such example. He refused absolutely to join in with anything we did. And he defied his tent leader, the Bosun, and even me, time and time again. He had to go! And go he did! Actually, there were two lads who left us prematurely through "unsuitability".

The self-inflicted injury was the result of ignoring my instruction to everyone: Do not run downhill.

The lad sustained a very severe injury to his left knee, which caused him to be hospitalised for the best part of a week.

Here are two (word for word) witness statements from lads who were with the injured boy. I am only using their initials:

*Accident to A.P.: 29 July 1994.*

*Statement from 'S.B.' (Tent Three).*

*I was standing with 'A', who said "Shall we run down the hill?"*

*I said "No, don't run," but he did.*

*Both members of staff told us not to run downhill.*

(Ironically, this was the lad who I ended up taking home on 3rd August).

This statement was witnessed and signed Barrie Gretton, chair of the committee, on Friday 29th July 1994.

---------------------------------------------------------

Statement from K.E (Tent Six, same tent as 'A')

*I was not very far up the hill, and 'A' was with me. He started to run down the hill, but couldn't stop. He got even faster, and slipped, doing a double somersault.*

*He got up and I saw he had cut his knee. Then he bent it, and it opened up.*

This statement was witnessed and signed by John Preece (staff member).

---------------------------------------------------------

The children were all given sound advice and instruction by me before they left Camp, and one of the most important issues was how to enjoy the hills, and keep safe, and free from unnecessary injury. Unfortunately, 'A' chose to disregard all attempts to stop him running down the hill; and paid a hefty price!

This is the list of staff and children for Camp 1994:

Alan Scriven (Skipper), Steff Latewood (Bosun), Wendy Smith (QM), John Preece (Cook), David Scriven (Kitchen).

Part-time help: Owen Lewis (Ghost), Alan Preece, Tony Hammond.

In the tents:

Tent One: Leader Nicky Piggott, Michael Pargeter (Assistant), Daniel Jones, David James, Aaron Jordan, Ryan Griffiths, Jamie Preece, Carl Fitzgibbon, Armadeep Jhangra, Wayne Cook, John Sutherland.
Tent Two: Leader Dean Nightingale, Sean Davis, Carl Brain, Daniel Grizzle, Ben Stuart, Chris Millinson, Lee Davies, Michael Dwyer, Daniel Davies, John Locke.
Tent Three: Leader Phil Woods, Andrew Foxall, Joseph Parkes, S.B., Peter Newton, Paul Kelly, Mathew Guest, Steven Guest, Errol Jones.
Tent Four: Leader Richard George, Gary Grant, Bobby Grant, Barry Bunn, Andrew Nash, Damien Readman, David Readman, Ben Morris, Mathew Allen.
Tent Five: Leader Steve Phillips, Mathew Grant, Anthony Moffatt, Paul Moffatt, Wade Davies, Andrew Ledbury, Tom Scriven, Terence Biddle.
Tent Six: Leader Marc Scriven, Dave Shaw (Assistant), Steven Johnson, Lee Johnson, Wayne James, Simon Guest, Christopher Brown, Mathew Brown, Andrew Locke, AP**, Carl Evers.
**Involved in an accident off Camp. (See below).

Wade Davies came to my notice for a completely different reason: he was the best footballer we had seen at Camp to date. I absolutely loved the Camp football matches, whether it was the inter-tent competitions, or our regular staff-versus-the-lads matches. Most of the Camp would join in, and we would even rope in visitors when the opportunity arose. So naturally, being pretty useful with a football (he says), I could identify any equally (or even more) talented players, especially amongst the boys. Many were the times I upset the cook, JP mainly, because I wouldn't call an abrupt end to a game when a meal was ready. He always forgave me, though!

I mentioned above that a couple of lads left us early. I felt a wisp of failure, to be honest, when I took the decision to let them go home. One of them was a member of Dean Nightingale's group; so really, there's no need for me, Dean or anyone of us at Camp that year to feel bad. No one could have tried harder than Dean to get him to stay; the lad just wasn't cut out for "Camp life", and neither was S.B., who was collected from Camp.

Throughout the Camp's early history (from 1959 to 1997), Bill and I endeavoured at all times to ensure the children had a brilliant holiday. We never tried to change them (one of the reasons why we hardly viewed the case histories); we were there, with the voluntary staff, to care for the lads to the very best of our ability, which was considerable for most of us (based on the years we were at Camp). And for the overwhelming majority of our charges, the opinion was that we succeeded, overwhelmingly!

I visited the lad who had injured himself while he was in Royal Shrewsbury Hospital and he told me he was very sorry for running down the hill after being told he mustn't. I said he was not to worry, and if it was at all possible (I knew it wasn't, but the boy was upset about missing out) he could come back to us if his mother was ok with that, and his knee was healed. He had in fact caused himself a serious injury which, according to his mother's solicitors, required a general anaesthetic to clean and treat.

I also spoke to the lad's mother, explaining everything to her in as much detail as I had to hand. She accepted, initially, that it was simply an accident of A's own making.

As far as we (Camp committee) were concerned, after my conversation with her, A's mother had accepted the fact that her son's accident was a result of him ignoring my instructions whilst on Camp, and those of his tent leaders out in the valley. Imagine my horror when I received the following correspondence from a Dudley WRVS Children's Holiday Organiser. I have chosen not to include the personal details of those involved:

*Date: 19 Sept 1994*

*Dear Alan,*

*I have received the enclosed letter from Dudley Social Services. As you can see; unfortunately A's mother has approached a solicitor about the accident at Camp.*

*I have written to DSS and clarified the situation regarding my telephone call to Miss P (bottom of first page of solicitor's letter) and explained that I heard from you on Saturday morning (30 July) about the accident; that you told me it was a serious injury, and that I then contacted Miss P and went to see her and gave her £100 for travel expenses. I have also explained to DSS that we only recruit children for the Camp and that I don't have detailed information about organisation, numbers of leaders and children or the incident itself, so I have passed the solicitor's letter to you for you to provide the details they are requesting.*

*I have confirmed that Miss P did sign a medical consent form for treatment to be authorised by the holiday organisers.*

*I would be grateful if you could contact the solicitors direct with any relevant information. I am very sorry that Miss P has felt it necessary to pursue the matter further.*

Below is the solicitor's letter the WRVS passed on to me:

*Dear Madam*

*<u>OUR CLIENT MISS P.</u>*

*We have been consulted by the above named in connection with an accident to her son ... on Friday 29 July at the beginning of a Camping holiday arranged by the WRVS.*

*Information received by Miss P from any source in connection with this incident is extremely limited, however, according to our instructions, 'A' was delivered by her to the WRVS ... at 12 noon on Friday 29 July. She believes that five adults were in charge of the party but is unaware of the number of children involved.*

*Between 8 and 9pm that night, her neighbour received a telephone call and called Miss P to the telephone. She was informed that 'A' had met with an accident, was in the Royal Shrewsbury Hospital, and that she should attend asap. Miss P explained that she was without money, and was unable to borrow any but that her sister was coming to visit her the following day from London and may be able to take her to Shrewsbury.*

*Later that same evening ... a contact with the WRVS also telephoned and asked if Miss P had any money to attend the hospital. It was suggested during this conversation that the WRVS would pay £100 for travel expenses. You will appreciate that this was before Miss P had been given any details of the nature of the accident to her son and his condition. The following day ... (WRVS) attended our client's home and gave her*

[page 2 starts with the following:]

*At about 6pm the following day Miss P arrived at the RSH with her sister and was shocked and distressed to find her son clearly in a great deal of pain, and on an intravenous drip. She was informed by the paediatrician that he had a "nasty gash" on his knee-cap and had to undergo a general anaesthetic for the wound to be cleaned. He would stay in hospital for a minimum five days. In fact, XX was discharged after three days. His discharge was of a somewhat distressing event in that Miss P received a telephone call from the hospital asking her to go and fetch her son. She was unable to do so but a Social Worker in the event, gave her a lift to the hospital. Unfortunately, unbeknown to Miss P, by that time the hospital had already arranged for 'A' to be taken back to Dudley, where he was left with a neighbour.*

*You will appreciate that Miss P has been much distressed by the sequence of events and we are writing to you because we understand that although the holiday was arranged by the WRVS, it was at your suggestion, so presumably you have some relevant information.*

*Are you able to assist us on the following points :-*
*Please let us know who was responsible for arranging the holiday and identify the person or persons responsible at the Camp.*
*Are you able to let us have any idea of the number of children involved and the number of supervising staff?*
*Are you able to give us any information as to what exactly happened to 'A'? Miss P was originally informed that he had been running and tumbled down a hill. 'A' himself has told his mother that he in fact fell off a rope.*

*We trust you will be able to assist us on the above points. You will appreciate our client's distress. It had been recommended to her that 'A' would benefit from this Camping holiday, and it would seem that within hours of his departure from Dudley, her son was undergoing an operation under general anaesthetic as a result of an injury. We have to say that we were also rather concerned about this, but Miss P believes that she did sign an authority for any medical treatment to be authorised by the holiday organisers. Are you able to confirm this please?*

So... who'd be a volunteer? Lots of us, thankfully!

My initial thoughts: having received the letter from the WRVS and a copy of the solicitor's correspondence to them, to try and make contact with Bill Williams. He would know what to do. I was very concerned, to be honest... for myself and my (to date) successful record, but more so for the continuation of the Longmynd Adventure Camp. Something like this, I considered, could finish it for good! And it would happen on my watch! Thirty-six years of happy, successful Camps could end by the hand of this one incident! Then I thought: if I phone Bill and he actually agrees to speak to me, I'm admitting failure when it absolutely wasn't my fault. Then I considered ringing Pat H. She would help me through this apparent developing nightmare. But then I remembered that she wasn't too well. Did I want to burden her? Absolutely not!

After much consideration, and without speaking to another soul about it, I decided to seek the help of my fellow committee colleague, His Honour Judge Peter Northcote. Peter was a good man, whom I considered a friend. I had spent weekends at his lovely home, when he and his wife Pat lived at Crosshouses, Shrewsbury. Peter was my choice of “defence counsel”.

Two days after the correspondence came into my hands, I contacted Peter. I told him the truth; everything that had happened, and that the lad had lied to his mother about how he had sustained such an awful injury. I also told him that I had taken witness statements which had been independently witnessed, that I had informed all the relevant people/authorities at my earliest convenience, and I had visited the boy in hospital; he had apologised for what he had done to cause his injury, and asked, nay pleaded, to be allowed back at Camp. My final words to Peter were to inform him of the staff to children ratio.

He advised me to send all correspondence and information I held on this business (as he referred to it), including the lad’s WRVS report (case history), to him immediately, and that he would be back in touch as soon as he could.

Peter did get back to me and told me to forget it; he had dealt with it. I would hear no more about it. The matter was closed. There would be no repercussions as far as blame was concerned, and it would not affect my position as Skipper. To say I was relieved is a gross understatement! It brought a satisfying close to the worst Camp of my whole time with the charity.

Camp ’94 brought me to the decision to hold a meeting (in November) with all personnel connected to the LAC. The aim was, and I make no apologies now, as I made none back then, to secure a vote of confidence in my style of leadership. And if I won that vote I would continue running the Camp as I saw fit and make any changes (to staff or otherwise) I deemed necessary. I did win the vote and as a result I made some changes, which I announced at the committee AGM which took place on 22nd Jan 1995. Here is a resumé:

I wrote to Annie Williams – not Bill's daughter – (see book one), thanking her for all her previous help; adding that I would not be requiring any further assistance. As it happens, however, she did return, but only for the final get-together in 1998.

I decided that the 1995 Camp dates would be from 27th July to 7th August inc. with a maximum of thirty boys (20 from West Midlands; 10 from Shropshire).

No child must have had his 13th birthday (this was due to the bad behaviour of most of the older boys on Camp '94).

As far as possible, all beneficiaries would be attending Camp for the first time, as agreed with WRVS.

Everything was agreed and accepted; we move on...

It is worth saying here that the reader may remember from my first book that Bill called a meeting in the Skipper's caravan on an autumn evening back in 1989. His intention was to win a vote of confidence to run the Camp as he saw fit. The only difference between Bill's meeting and mine was that I was prepared to discuss my reasons for calling said meeting and unfortunately Bill had not been open to the same with his.

# Chapter Twelve

The following year, 1995, began on a rather sad note, when I received the following letter from Pat H, exactly one year before her death at 83 years old.

*Dear Alan*

*You will be aware that I have been, and still am, ill. I have been given the "gypsy's warning", and must take things easily.*

*This I have done for a week; all I have done is wash up. My neighbours and friends have been very kind, busy shopping for me, and bringing me meals.*

*I have written to Barrie and Don, saying I will resign from the LAC committee - but shall always maintain my interest in the Camp.*

*I felt that I must write to you, because you and I have known each other longer than anyone else now working for the Camp. Even though I am told that John has resigned, and said it was because the Camp "was going backward not forward", you and I know different, don't we?*

*When I look at our present premises; flush toilets, running drinking water, and a roomy well-equipped kitchen, and think back to the water tank which had to be filled at the stand-pipe in Minton. The bucket lavatories - that awful unhygienic kitchen.......!!!!!*

*When I took over as cook, the teapot from the previous year's Camp had not even been emptied!*

*So you and I know that we have come a long way forward, don't we!*

*Whoever takes over as cook this year should find an immaculate kitchen, and will, I am sure, leave an immaculate kitchen for the next people to use it.*

*It is good to know, that because of this, we are able to raise a bit more income by way of letting the Camp out.*

*It is good to hear that the staffing situation looks promising for this year; will you please give them all my thanks and very best wishes for a good Camp. And I hope we get a set of good children this year that will be happier for having come to Camp. That is what it's all about.*

*So much of the success of the Camp rests on your shoulders, Alan.*

*You will, I know, do as you have always done; your very best. All being well, I'll come to Camp.*

*With every good wish to you personally*

*Sincerely,*

*Pat.*

Pat's final letter to me mentions the fact that we "let" the premises during the year when our Camps weren't operative. And as she says, the extra income was greatly appreciated. Her point about the Camp being in much better condition now, is borne out by the following correspondence - written on 30th May 1995 - to committee member Don Rogers. It came from Mr Mike Saull of Meole Brace Lions, Shrewsbury:

*Dear Don*

*Just a short note to accompany the keys I forgot to leave with you, to say thanks for letting us hire the Long Mynd site for our annual Camp.*

*While at the Camp we received a visit from the District Commissioner for Cubs and his assistant - attached is the form they have to fill in. While not all the comments are directly relevant - they couldn't have scored the site and the facilities higher!*

*Cheers*

*Mike Saull*

My decision to exclude people who had given their free time voluntarily for a good number of years was, I concede, a very risky thing to do. Especially when getting the right kind of help was usually achieved through the suggestion of experienced helpers, and the people I chose to manage without in 1995 were such people. That said, my mind was set, and my conscience was clear.

Wendy Smith took responsibility for cooking our meals, and whilst she herself would readily admit to being nowhere near the standard John had set, nevertheless she did a very acceptable job;

one hundred per cent, in fact, better than the previous person to replace John (for one year) back in the eighties!

Over the years since I had first been given the responsibility of acquiring the staff, I would like to think I did a reasonable job. Obviously one or two fell by the wayside after just one Camp, but many of them returned year on year as and when commitments allowed. Experience taught me who I could depend on to give us their time for the duration; who would be with us for the weekdays only, or weekends if required. One also had a good idea who would be available to stay behind to help with the clear-up... there weren't many of them, truth to tell. But the ones that did remain stayed till the very end! And these were the people who were first to be asked to help when the time came to start putting a group together for the next Camp, because as a rule, if someone was available to help right up till the Skipper left, they would also, in almost every case, arrive no later than the Thursday morning (set-up day).

Credit has to be given to Skipper Bill Williams whenever the topic of staffing arises, because in the very early dawn of his wonderful idea to give lads with a similar background to mine a holiday in the countryside, there was no precedence; no clues as to who would be suitable... and who wouldn't! Having said that, though, he was a police officer, and also the founder of Wistanstow Youth Club, so perhaps he did have an inkling at least who he could ask to help; fellow police officers were high on his "hopeful" list. Bill told me, however, that most of the ones who had initially agreed changed their mind once they found out that giving Bill a week or so would be taken from their annual leave.

One person who did answer Bill's call was a sixteen-year-old Craven Arms lad called Mike Powell. Mike had been a member of Bill's youth club in 1965, and he accepted Bill's invitation to join his staff for that year's "WVS Boys Camp". As you will know from my previous books, 1965 was also my first year at Camp, as a beneficiary of Bill's outstanding kindness to children in my position.

I remember Mike as a very fit young man; extremely likeable, and very eager to do well in order to repay Bill's faith in him. And how he succeeded! It actually verges on tragedy that Mike wasn't a part of this fantastic roller-coaster for longer than the years that he was involved!

Kids flocked to him as soon as the bus driver opened the door at the narrow lane junction of Minton Batch. I was never lucky enough to be a "fully paid-up member" of Mike's magical group, year on year, but he was always very nice to me, my brothers, and everyone else. And I have Mike to thank (in part) for my 33-year association with the Camp.

Through the "wonders" of modern-day technology, and social media, I have actually got Mike back in my life, after an absence of almost forty-five years. He's not the only one, either; there are at least half a dozen more old friends from back in our "Camp days" during the swinging sixties who are now an important part of my life, many of whom come to the monthly meetings I have mentioned. I'll talk more about these special friends as we move further along this unique path. But for now, I want to tell you a little bit about my good friend Mike; and how his life has panned out during the years that have come and gone since I knew him at Camp.

Mike's final year at Camp was 1972. He almost always managed to get Bill to appoint him leader of Tent Two; something Mike is still very proud of to this day. He got himself married, and that unfortunately put paid (as it did with others over the years) to his involvement with what became the Longmynd Adventure Camp. I count myself very fortunate that I was never embroiled in an "it's the Camp or me" situation!

Mike's employment included Farmore Farmers, and J.P. Woods of Craven Arms. He also joined the Royal Monmouthshire Engineers, and later became a part-time member of Craven Arms Fire Service. Quite a distinguished working career, I think you will agree.

As I mentioned, Mike was a member of Wistanstow Youth Club. He was also a founder member of a youth club in his home town of Craven Arms (mirroring Bill's achievement in some small way), which lasted in his words "for a long time."

These days, Mike is married to Diana, a lovely lady, and they live in Shrewsbury with their pet Staffordshire bull terrier, Angel, in glorious retirement... Mike, that is. Diana still works in a local care home.

It isn't lost on me, how fortunate I was to be the only person (aside from Bill) to attend Camp year after year when I was a part of it. And for that I have to thank my bosses at the companies I worked for during my years as a member of Bill's staff. There were one or two "close shaves", however, when I had to stand firm, but no real problems to speak of, if one doesn't count the two jobs I lost through sticking to my guns!

The 1995 Camp began on Wednesday 26th July. I finished work at the Midland Red bus depot in Wellington at 4pm and jumped into the driver's seat of the minibus the company had kindly lent me. As I was driving away, however, I was stopped by Peter Ralphs, the depot manager. He gave me the bad news that the company had not been able to get any insurance on the vehicle!

"Just one more problem to add to the others", I wrote in the Camp logbook; the others included a lack of help to set up. But we managed, as we always did. And by the time the lads arrived on the Friday, I was blessed with a good group of leaders and staff. Our first-night party went very well, with a "healthy" number of guests. It was always good to have as many people attend our first nights as we could get, because most of them weren't shy about dipping into their pockets to buy raffle tickets, make donations, or buy drinks (we always got a licence to sell alcohol at Camp).

Owen Lewis, sadly, couldn't be with us for this Camp, but did manage to attend the party. He suggested that we auction off the raffle prizes, after the first one had been called, thereby making more money. Owen himself conducted the auction and, true to his promise, we netted in excess of £100 from his extremely well-performed auction.

For this Camp (which I couldn't possibly have known would be my last as Skipper until 1997), Alan Preece, whom I had re-instated as Bosun, and I decided to promote my eldest son Marc to third in the pecking order. The idea was to ensure coverage of senior staff, should the events that led me to skipper the Camp back in 1979 re-occur. And also, we were looking towards the future, being unaware of course that there wasn't one!

The tents again proved successful, and not only for the fact that we had to wake the boys up most mornings; it was always nice when it worked this way round, and something we had got used to, to be honest.

The weather was brilliant, thus making life easier for everyone, and the twenty-eight children were a pleasure to be with. The whole Camp was so much better than the previous year's. There were no rows, or even disagreements; everyone did their own job and other work if I, the Bosun, or Marc asked them to. We gave Marc (whom we had given the title of "Swizzle" because Wendy Smith had gone to town to buy him a whistle but returned with a sweetie one... called a Swizzle) more and more responsibility as his confidence grew. The staff and the children gave him tremendous support, as did the Bosun and I. Marc was still only nineteen years old when I appointed him to assist Alan, but had in fact been a constant member of Camp since 1979, when still not three years of age! I have written in more detail the reason for Marc's early start in my first book so, suffice to say here, he was more than suitably experienced to tackle the added responsibility.

We were again lucky to be invited to Manor Adventure Camp, and on Tuesday 1st August, as well as taking a party of twelve boys to the Camp, I took a case of beer (provided by Don Rogers) for the Camp leader, Gareth Price, as a small thank you gesture.

It was a brilliant Camp, and we had lots of fun as a whole group, on numerous occasions. One being the day Alan Preece decided that he had a "dual personality" (the things we did to entertain the children sometimes verged on the ridiculous, but it always seemed to work). Alan shaved one side of his whole body, broke a pair of sunglasses in half, and even broke a plate in half. To add to this, he cut two of his outfits into opposite halves, painstakingly sewed them together, then put them on!

Picture the scene:

Marc had whistled for breakfast, and the lads stood at the entrance to the hall in their respective tent groups, waiting for him to send them inside. When everyone was in and at their tables, I told them that the Bosun would be joining us very soon, along with his "other half". The kitchen staff stood behind the counter waiting to serve up breakfast just as Alan walked in, with his half-glasses, half-plate, and half-and-half attire. Everyone in the hall (except Marc and me, because obviously we knew it was coming) was gobsmacked, initially, then as one, they exploded in laughter. Alan didn't bat an eyelid. He walked up to the counter and said, 'Morning from me and my brother Percy; I don't want porridge thanks, but Percy does.' He then held out his half a plate. My youngest son, Tom, was asked by Wendy to give "Percy" a small half-portion of porridge. As he did so, everyone was in stitches, even me and Marc. The Bosun turned and walked slowly through the hall, having a conversation with Percy:

'I thought you liked porridge?'

'I do, Percy, but not this morning, I'll have some bacon and tomato in a bit.'

'Good, because breakfast is important, Bosun.'

'Yes, I'm aware of that Percy, sit down and enjoy your porridge.'

And that was how it was for the rest of the day; brilliant fun, with all the lads and staff joining in, by talking to Percy and the Bosun as different people. Just a fantastic bunch of people enjoying being at Camp.

The only dampener was that the Campfire attendance was the lowest since my own time as a boy there.

Here's the full complement for 1995:

Staff: Alan Preece, Marc Scriven, Tom Scriven, David Scriven, Wendy Smith, and me.

Tent One: Leader Richard George. Damien Readman, Alan McSweeney, Daniel Ryng, Terry Biddle, Darren Powell-Bevan.

Tent Two: (Champions) Leader Dave Shaw. Ben Stewart, Michael Jones, Michael Duckett, James, Gary Owen.
Tent Three: Leader Michael Gaunt. Parvinder Suman, Michael O'Brien, Steven Johnson, Pele` Comrie, Lee Oulton, Scott Davies
Tent Four: Leader(s) Mel Drinkwater and Phil Woods. Stuart Brough, Gary Brough, Lee-Jay Comrie, Timothy Brittain, Jason Jennings, Jamie Preece (Alan's son).
Tent Five: Leader(s) Nicola Piggott and Steve Phillips. David Richards, Philip Hunnisett, Tommy Griffiths, Timmy Griffiths, Paul Southey.

There were four Michaels, three Alans, two Toms... but there's only one Pelè!

You might be wondering why the Bosun decided on the form of entertainment that he did for a few hours on that Sunday (6th August). It was actually a throwback to Skipper Williams' time at Camp.

During the eighties, Bill had formed his own security business, and as it was a newly formed company (from which his hard work eventually brought huge success), he needed to be available to all potential customers at all times. This meant that he had to, on occasions, change into a suit and go off to a meeting or whatever. He came out of his caravan one day, dressed immaculately, complete with cravat (Skipper liked his cravats) and headed for his car. A couple of the lads were milling around near the cars, and one said, 'You look nice, Skip, going to the pub?'

Quick as a flash, Skipper replied, 'I'm Skipper's twin brother, David, son, I've just come to borrow his car; will you tell him when he gets back please?'

Bill looked my way (I was by the hall doors) and gave me a sly wink, to which I responded, 'See you soon, David,' and then I called the lads to me so that the Skipper could safely reverse off the car park and proceed down the drive. I knew he was going out, but we hadn't rehearsed the "David" bit. And so it was for the remainder of that Camp; Skipper was visited now and again by his brother David, but strangely enough, they were never seen together!

Actually, that was another similarity Bill and I shared; we both had a brother called David (yes, David was a real brother of Bill's, but they weren't twins). Others included both being born into poor families, and Bill's dad dying when Bill was just a boy, whereas I never knew my dad – or of him, even – until it was too late!

My second marriage hit the rocks immediately following Camp '95; well, actually, it crashed into the rocks and shattered into a million pieces. It came as a shock because everything had seemed fine when Nicky left Camp at the end of the first-night party. And I'd spoken to her on the telephone a number of times whilst I was at Camp, and not once during those conversations did she even hint that we wouldn't have a marriage when I got back home. I tell a little more about this episode of my life in my first book; I only mention it now because as I again leaf through my substantial quantity of Camp memorabilia, I find the following correspondence (dated 19th September 1995) from Nicola Piggott, a valued member of my staff, and a good friend, too:

*Dear Alan*
*I would normally start, that I hope you're feeling well but obviously in the circumstances, you're not.*

*I'm not really sure what I can say - but I hope that healthwise, you're keeping ok.*

*What can I say - apart from if you want to talk I'm here (at least I will be from 30th Sept - I'm off to France on Thursday) but if you want to talk before, then give me a call at work (inc. Thursday morning).*

*I won't presume, or ask you anything here. This is just a note to say that I am thinking about you, and if you want to talk/a hug, I'm here.*
*Look after yourself*
*Nicky x*

I don't suppose it will surprise anyone when I say I didn't ring her, or go to see her. It wasn't because I didn't appreciate Nicky's lovely letter, I did, very much. But at the time, I couldn't have spoken to anyone about what was occupying my mind during those few weeks between finding out (firsthand) that my wife had been seeing someone else, and me leaving the marital home... her home! But nevertheless, it was a nice gesture from Nicky.

As far as Camp was concerned, what I went home to couldn't have been a bigger contrast! We had a fantastic time in every respect. Kim Harris of Shropshire WRVS sent me this note a short time after Camp:

*Dear Alan*

*Just a few lines to say thank you for another wonderful Camp.*

*As part of our negotiations with Social Services (and hoped for partnership) we've devised an evaluation form to show how much the children enjoy various aspects of camping.*

*Of the eleven boys who filled in the forms, you'll be delighted to hear that to the question "How would you describe your holiday to your friends?"*

*Eight said Brilliant; two thought "Very good".*

*I'm sure you will agree that this confirms what we already knew.*

*I look forward to seeing you all again next year.*

*Kind Regards*

*Kim*

It was always good to know that the lads had enjoyed

themselves. It gave us a sense of achievement, if you will; a definite reason to continue. Their letters, too, were a massive bonus; every single one was positive.

But the whole situation was moving slowly (at first) towards an irreversible change. A change that would render the Longmynd Adventure Camp redundant, in as much as the purpose it was created for was being chipped away by a growing desire from our up-till-now loyal sponsors, to steer a different course as far as holidays for children was concerned. And I have to say, judging from the committee's lacklustre response when it all came to a head in 1998, it appeared to concur!

The end of the policies and format we had adhered to since the first Camp (proper) in 1959 was staring us full in the face. But we couldn't see it... yet!

Then, to make matters worse, along came 1996!

The Camp, in itself, was successful, under the circumstances. But the year began on a very sad note, and got progressively worse!

On 11th February, Mrs Hetty Williams (wife of our Camp's founder) passed away. I didn't learn of this wonderful lady's passing for quite a while, due to the ongoing ill-feeling (to say the least) towards me from Bill, after what had happened at the beginning of the decade. For that reason, I wasn't able to send my condolences to Bill and the family, much less attend the funeral. It hit me hard when I eventually found out. Mrs Williams (I never once addressed her differently) and I had enjoyed a nice friendship, which was rooted in the mid-to-late sixties, when I was a regular weekend visitor to the Williams household in Shrawardine, Shrewsbury. She was absolute gold dust; just a very nice lady, with a fantastic personality, whom I took to from the very first time I met her. It wouldn't have hurt Bill (I think) to at least let me know. He could have said I wasn't welcome at the house or the funeral service, but if he had just told me, I would have been able to go and pay my respects afterwards. That hurt me more than I've ever let on. And there was an obvious message contained in Bill's silence: *I don't want anything more to do with you, Alan!*

Back in the mid-eighties, Bill opened a shop in Old Coleham, Shrewsbury. Since his retirement in 1973 from the West Mercia Constabulary, on health grounds (a blood clot on the lung), he was in the security business - following a spell as a representative for Evans Publishers - selling items of security for the home, and working premises. His shop was (at first) a one-person business operation, which was fine until Bill needed to be elsewhere for whatever reason. I mentioned in my previous book(s) that (in 1986) he actually offered me an equal partnership in his growing business, prior to taking on the shop premises; I couldn't afford the six hundred pounds asking price though, sadly. I say sadly because of how our friendship was to spectacularly collapse just a few short years later. If we had been business partners, I feel I might have been able to talk to Bill about what divided us at the end of the eighties/early nineties.

A situation arose which meant that Bill had to be away from the shop for a whole week. He asked me if I would look after it for him, opening up, serving potential customers, and closing at 5.00 pm from the Monday through till Friday. Luckily, I was able to get a week's holiday from work, so all that was left to do was get Tina's okay. Actually, that was never going to be a problem; our marriage didn't encompass those sorts of "conditions" where one had to get the other's permission to do things separately from the other partner (within reason, obviously). Nevertheless, it was only right and proper, and fair to make sure she didn't have a problem with me disappearing for a few days. She didn't, so I rang Bill.

He was delighted. I was nervous. He said I would be fine. I doubted it. He reminded me that I was familiar with most of the products in the shop, because I had done door-to-door selling with him as and when I could help him. I felt better.

'It's going to be five very long days, though, Bill, with all the travelling.'

'I thought you'd stay at our house, Alan. Hetty and Deb are looking forward to having you for the week.'

'Are you sure, Bill; they don't mind, really'

'Really, Alan, it's no problem, so is that a yes?'

'Yes, Bill. Thank you all very much.'

I then told Tina that I would actually be away from home from the Sunday until the weekend. She was fine about it, so I travelled to Bill's house on the Sunday evening.

Throughout that week, whilst I covered for Bill at the shop, and as a guest of Mrs Williams and Debbie, I was treated like a member of the family. Nothing was too much trouble. I slept on a sofa bed in Bill's study at their house in Meole Brace. Each evening, I was invited into the front room to watch a bit of television, and before retiring, Mrs Williams gave me a nice generous helping of Bill's finest single malt!

The meals, breakfast and evening, were delicious and filling. Mrs Williams even prepared some lunch for me to take to the shop. I was a little sorry to leave at the end of the week, if I am honest. I've never forgotten how kind she and Debbie were.

It wasn't the first time I had witnessed Mrs W's caring and kind personality. Back in 1980, during our very first time on the new and permanent site, my son Marc fell ill. I describe the reasons why Marc was with me again (1979 being his first experience of being away from his mom for a while) and why he became ill, in my first book. I also mention a most extraordinary experience I had one night in the tent I shared with Marc and Terry Pugh!

When it became obvious to me that Marc wasn't his usual bubbly self, I laid him down on one of the staffroom sofas so that I could keep an eye on him.

Whilst he was on the sofa, Mrs Williams arrived with Ann, Glyn (Ann's husband) and Debbie to see Bill, and us of course, as they regularly did. Skipper's wife asked about Marc, who was just a few days from his fourth birthday. I explained the situation and she immediately went to see him. It was nothing serious; he was just "under the weather". Mrs Williams asked me if she could take him home with her to "get him right". I said yes; Marc, however, said no! He wouldn't go with Skipper's good wife for love nor money. So she told me she would come to Camp every day to look after him until he was better. How nice and considerate. A truly lovely lady, with absolutely no airs and graces. Her calm and unshakeable demeanour, together with solid support for everything Bill did, absolutely allowed him focus on whatever "project" he became involved in, both in his personal life and his public duties as a police officer. She was an unsung hero in every sense of the phrase.

Hetty's father originated from Dartford. He worked in the leather and shoe trade, which meant he had to move around the country to look for work. His travels brought him to Leicester, where the family settled for a while; Hetty was born there in 1927, as was her sister Marjorie two years earlier. The family moved again, to Donnington in Shropshire. In the fullness of time, Marjorie returned to Leicester, where she married.

To digress a little: in my earlier book, I mention playing one of the "ghosts of Minton Batch", opposite a new tent leader called John Clarke. He became the most "famous" of the ghosts, after his unexpected compromise to a situation he had unknowingly engineered himself before taking up his position at his designated point and commencing his "walk" towards me and the children. John was Marjorie's son. Sadly, he passed away some years ago.

Bill and Hetty met when they were both sixteen years old. Hetty was living in Donnington and Bill in Wellington. She worked at Bates & Hunt Chemist shop in Trench. Their eldest daughter Ann tells me that her dad, apparently, introduced her mom to smoking, which back then was a favourite pastime of many folk.

They married in Wellington in 1948; shortly afterwards, Bill joined the police force, and was (a little while after training) posted to Bridgnorth, where Ann was born in 1950.

A further posting in 1954 took the family to Wistanstow, in South Shropshire. This is where Bill got his "calling" to become the founder of the Longmynd Adventure Camp. Ann remembers the police house they lived in as being busy almost all of the time. Youth club members (such as Mick Powell, and Terry Pugh who I mention in book one) seemed to be there very often, making canoes and the like. People arrived regularly with lost dogs, bicycles they had found, etc.

Ann also talks of one or two old cars which her dad had acquired being in the garden from time to time. Another acquisition of Bill's was a motorbike and side-car. Ann remembers him riding it to Borth with the family for a caravan holiday; Hetty riding pillion, with Ann, her grandmother, and Bonny their pet golden retriever in the side car! I remember Bonny from when I used to stay with Bill, Mrs Williams and Debbie, who was born in 1960... or was it a later Bonny I remember? Ann said there were a few Bonnies over the years.

When Debbie was a little girl, she had to be taken by ambulance to Shrewsbury once a week for physiotherapy. Her mother escorted her, and was travel-sick in the back of the ambulance on almost every occasion. As a result of their regular trips to Shrewsbury, Hetty got to know the crew and attendants very well. And when a position became vacant on the ambulances, Hetty was asked if she would like to apply for it. She did, was successful, and never sick again following her "upgrading" to the front of the ambulance!

When the family moved from Wistanstow to number ten Shrawardine, Shrewsbury, Hetty went to work as an auxiliary nurse at Shelton Hospital, remaining there until 1970, which was the time that Debbie had her operation. Hetty then got herself a position at Woolworths.

It would be impossible to find anyone who didn't like and admire Mrs Williams. I am truly honoured to be able to say that she was a good friend to me, at all times. I was very sorry to lose that friendship when my close association with her husband came to a dramatic and bitter end (for six or so years) in 1989.

I don't know, obviously, what Mrs Williams made of my fall-out with Bill. Her devout loyalty to her husband ensured that she would never have attempted to contact me for my version of the events which culminated in such a harsh finale to our (up till then) "father/son" friendship. But I am certain of this: if (and it's a big if, because I doubt Bill would have told her in any detail about what had gone on) she had been aware of the facts, she would have at least considered that maybe it wasn't all down to me. God bless you, Mrs W, and thank you for everything!

In my humble opinion, there are six ladies to whom the Longmynd Adventure Camp should always be incredibly grateful, to this day!

**Mrs Hetty Williams.** As described above, provided unlimited and undivided loyalty and support to Bill, which enabled him to realise his dream of building a lasting legacy, to enrich the lives of less fortunate children, up and down the country; truly, the most august of ladies.

**Mrs Robin Hazlerigg.** The WVS Chief Children's Holiday Organiser at the time of Bill's first steps into giving socially deprived kids a country break. She was Bill's rock when it came to whatever the WVS could do to assist Bill in making it very successful; not least, good sponsorship for each child.

**Mrs Marjorie Lathe** selected the children from the West Midlands to attend the Camp. A lovely lady, without whose involvement and dedication to her responsibilities I would not now be writing these words. She was responsible not only my selection from 1965 to 1967 inclusive but, most importantly perhaps, letting me go in 1968, when I was actually over the age insurance limit.

**Mrs Winnie Hull** offered herself as a cook on a number of Bill's early Camps on Jack Williams' field (that small piece of heaven I have mentioned throughout this trilogy of books). She was no "spring chicken", but lived on the field just like the rest of us, under canvas, and always seemed more than happy to be there. Mrs Hull, or "our Winnie" as she became known, was another WVS stalwart, and truly the salt of the earth. When Mrs Hull first agreed to come and cook for Bill, she was offered "digs" in Minton. She spent just one night in the hamlet before saying to Skipper: 'If sleeping under canvas is good enough for everyone else, then it's certainly good enough for me.'

**Mrs H.M. Hazlehurst QPM.** Pat H is featured throughout my books, and rightly so. She was with Bill from the Camp's very early beginnings, and an original committee member. During her many years as part of the Camp, Pat did a great deal to prove her worth to it, and to Bill, and certainly to the many hundreds of young lads who were lucky enough (and I mean that in the nicest of ways) to be selected for a holiday at this magical wonderland.

**Mrs Kim Harris** was one of the WRVS escorts whose commitment to, and enthusiasm for, the Camp went a long way in helping make it a success. And it would be most unfair not to mention Kim's husband, Gordon. I met Kim and Gordon (she was never without him) very early into my tenure as Skipper. They always arrived at about lunchtime on the first day, with a few lads, some of whom may have been there previously; others who were coming for the first time. Initially, Kim asked if it would be okay if she and Gordon "hung around for a bit", to ease her lads into Camp life. There was no problem with that request, or the others that were put to us throughout the duration of the holiday, and indeed, over the years. Kim and Gordon proved their worth to the Camp on every occasion that they joined us. We established that they would be very welcome at any time; indeed, Gordon was even asked to help out as a daytime tent leader sometimes, and his assistance and willingness were never more appreciated than in 1992, when we were almost overcome by a stomach bug that viciously raked through the Camp! Gordon became a part-time leader of Cabin Four.

On the final day of Camp, having stayed till the last on the previous night (Campfire night), they would be back with us bright and early, to assist with the breaking of Camp, before escorting the lads they had brought back to their homes.

Obviously, there were more ladies, over the Camp's first forty years, for whom a mention is most certainly warranted, including, and in no order of preference:

Mrs Pat Northcote, who raised a considerable amount of money (over many years) along with her husband (and a fellow committee colleague of mine) His Honour Judge Peter Northcote.

Mrs Eileen Mansell was, in her time, a cook on Camp for a few years; assisted usually by her friend Mrs Pat Irving. They were Church Stretton ladies and the wives of Don and Brian respectively; both of whom were tent leaders during my time as a child on Camp.

Mrs Diane Williams was the wife of Roy "Butcher" Williams. Diane assisted Roy when he took his turn at doing the cooking (or maybe he assisted her). Both of them were close friends of Bill's, and helpers on Camp for many, many years.

Ms Nicola Piggott (Nicky) joined us as a tent leader in 1991. She was quality; one of the best leaders I ever worked with. Camp was, I think, new to Nicky (meaning she hadn't done anything like it previously). But she took to it like the proverbial duck to water. A while after my involvement with the Camp was over, Nicky contacted me and invited me out for a meal; we were friends anyway, having done the occasional hike over "the Mynd" and the like, so I agreed to meet her in Sedgley. During the meal, she mentioned that she had joined the LAC committee. She asked me if I minded; in other words, did I see her as a traitor of sorts, perhaps. I sincerely hope I convinced her on that night that nothing of the sort had or would ever come into my mind. I left the committee of my own free will, after the debacle with the WRVS chief Children's Holiday Organiser from 1998 in Manchester soon into his "reign". The committee, as is fully documented in my first book, gave me not one scrap of support, when I needed it most, so I took the decision, rightly or wrongly, to sever all contact with the charity. I can't say the Camp, because however one tries to dress it up, Camp was finished; dead in the water! It has never since 1997 operated as it was originally intended to. But if Nicky thought that her joining the committee might be of benefit to it, then that was her decision, and none of my business.

Mrs Joanna Roundell-Greene was holidaying in All Stretton in 1981. I bumped into her in the lane between our new site and Minton Batch. I was with a group of lads. Jo asked a lot of questions about the Camp, and after I had answered her, she said she was interested in coming along to “have a look”. She did come, and was very impressed; so much so that she paid us more visits throughout the week. Jo attended our Campfire with her then husband Phil Pinniger, and at the end of the evening told Bill she would like to come again the following year. I stayed in touch with her and, true to her word, she came back in 1982 and helped us on a daily basis, whilst Phil offered his services as a full-time tent leader, taking charge of Tent Two.

Phil’s help ended, however, when he and Jo divorced, but Jo continued to help out, and even became a member of the committee, taking the role of Secretary. As I said in my first book, Jo arranged a fundraising charity football match between (her friend) the actor Dennis Waterman’s celebrity XI and a team of former Wolves stars, headed by Derek Dougan.

Wendy Smith was a prison officer; a Yorkshire lass who was full of fun, and a fantastic member of staff. During her years as a very valued helper, Wendy filled the positions of tent leader, and QM (or Bursar). I have nine photograph albums of Camp history, the later ones with numerous pictures of Wendy. You won’t find one of them showing Wendy without a big smile on her face!

If any one of us, child or adult, was “under the weather”, Wendy looked after us. She would assess our situation; usually nothing more than mild symptoms of whatever, and then either drive into town for some appropriate medication after a chat to the pharmacist, or cart us off to the local GP. In 1992, when we had that awful stomach bug, Wendy Smith was an absolute diamond, with no “inclusions”!

Christine Harte (Tina to family and close friends) was my wife for thirteen years. She is featured in some detail in my first book, but I just wanted to include her in this group of ladies who in their own particular way helped the Camp to prosper. This will sound a little weird, but we divorced “accidentally” in 1988, having been separated for the previous twelve months. I won’t elaborate on any of that stuff except to say we are the “exception to the rule”, in that we have remained on good terms; good friends, to be exact, ever since we split. I always said that although we did get divorced, our kids never realised... well they did, obviously, but you know what I mean. No rows whatsoever; we’ve always looked out for each other, as friends do. In fact, since our divorce we have, when circumstances dictated, shared a home, as we do today, and this is the fourth time of doing so!

What I wanted to say is that without Tina’s full support for my Camp commitments, I doubt very much whether I would have progressed through the ranks and continued to be a part of Camp year after year. In my own experience, there have been a good many potentially brilliant tent leaders/helpers who have, fallen by the wayside as a result of family commitments. No names, no pack drill, as the saying goes.

I have been very lucky, and that fact, as I have said before, is not lost on me.

So 1996 got off on a sad note, even though I wasn't aware of Mrs Williams' passing. And this poor start was compounded by the subsequent passing of Pat H on 26th April.

On 4th May, I wrote to the Rural Dean of Shrewsbury, who was to officiate at Pat's funeral, asking if it would be possible to speak at the service, on behalf of the LAC. Below is his reply (dated 9th May), which I fully accepted:

*Dear Mr Scriven*

*Thank you for your letter of the 4 May in which you write in such a glowing and affectionate manner to the memory of Pat Hazlehurst. I totally agree with all your sentiments as to what a remarkable lady she was and can fully understand your wish to speak about her in appreciation of all that she has done for the Longmynd Adventure Camp, and for yourself.*

*I regretfully must decline your request to speak at the funeral service because as I am sure you are aware Pat was also involved in many other associations and activities - some of whom have expressed a similar wish. Therefore, being practical in the first instance and being cautious in the second, that I do not offend, by omission anyone, I feel only I, with all the information I have received from all areas and my own personal friendship with Pat, must try to share all our feelings when we come to think of her in the service.*

*I will endeavour to include as much of your information from your letter as I can during the address in the service and if there is anything else you wish to add, please telephone me as soon as possible.*

*I look forward to meeting you on 16 May*

*Yours sincerely*

*Rod Biddle*

*Revd R W D Biddle*

*Rural Dean of Shrewsbury*

My first books cover what Reverend Biddle said on behalf of us from the LAC at the service... and crucially, what happened after it!

My crass stupidity still haunts me, especially at times like this, when I am forced to re-live it! All I'll say here is that I was so looking forward to seeing Bill again, after years of being "out in the cold", as far as his life and friendship was concerned. I thought there might be a small chance of a crack in the ice, which could lead, eventually, to a thaw.

It is often said that situations caused by extreme action sometimes, in an odd sort of way, bring solutions to a long-held grudge, or even deep-rooted hatred and/or anger. This episode of our association (mine and Bill's) turned out, thankfully, be one such occasion; and I'm very that happy that it did!

On 7th June 1996, I wrote the following in the Camp's logbook:

*On 26th April this year, our "matriarch" Pat Hazlehurst passed away. It was very much unexpected and she will be very sadly missed. Pat was eighty-three years old. Her funeral on 16th May was attended by LAC representatives (Committee and Staff).*

*Our founder, my predecessor Bill Williams did not attend. This unfortunately produced a completely unnecessary reaction from me, in the form of a very nasty and disrespectful letter to him.*

*I later discovered the reason for his non attendance; he replied to me, saying he had been resident in the Royal Shrewsbury Hospital (coronary care ward) at the time of Pat's funeral.*

*I immediately sent Bill an unreserved apology, which he did not reply to**.*

*I was rightfully accused of "bringing the Camp into disrepute" (as my letter to Bill was written on a LAC letterhead), and as a result, I was stripped of my authority as Skipper until the end of the year.*

*I shall be at Camp however, in the position of tent leader, following an invitation by new Skipper Alan Preece. Marc Scriven becomes Bosun, and Wendy Smith as the third member of the senior staff.*

*Good luck and best wishes to all!*

*Alan Scriven.*

**I did eventually receive a letter from Bill, accepting my apology. My position, however, for that year at least, remained the same as detailed above; I would be at Camp as a tent leader. I fully accepted the committee's decision to "reduce me to the ranks" for Camp 1996.

In early July, I received a nice letter from Richard George, telling me he wouldn't be able to help at Camp this year. It was always a cause for mild concern when an expected member of staff informed us that they were unavailable; one just hoped that the others would be, and generally speaking they were.

My late friend Alan Preece and my eldest son Marc did a very acceptable job of running Camp '96, and I settled into a position I had not occupied since 1978, and to be honest, I thoroughly enjoyed it as I rolled back the years, getting into my stride immediately.

The first-night party was sufficiently attended to bring in a few more welcome pennies by way of raffles, etc. And Alan records in the log-book that Mrs Pat Northcote said she would bring an electric organ to Camp. This caused a bit of a surprise, if only for the fact that we had no one capable of playing it! Now if any one of Tina's maternal blood aunts and uncles had have been with us, if ever Pat had kept her promise, the organ would have never stopped being played, because all of them were accomplished players!

The children were late arriving on the Friday, and as a result it was 16:15 hours before they were eventually allocated to their tents. I was asked to be the leader of Tent Two. I agreed, and as I began walking towards the tent with my new group, I could have sworn I heard the dulcet tones of a voice from long ago... I could... it was the unmistakable sound of Mick Powell, from back in the day: *You'd better win the competition now, my boy; you're in charge of my tent.* I didn't let Mick, my boys, or myself, down!

The Skipper notes that it was very late by the time the lads got their heads down, due to a game of Harbour Light in the valley. He adds, however, that it didn't prevent them from rising at 05:15 hrs!

How do they do it?

By the second day, I was already setting the pace as far as the tent competition was concerned; all the old skills returning to assist me in making my tent group the one to look up to.

Alan mentions in the logbook that a couple of minor squabbles surfaced on the Saturday, but were quickly forgotten (as usual). He adds, though, that "interference from the kitchen staff doesn't help". Some things never changed!

The weather hadn't been too kind to us so far, but at least the lads were able to enjoy a few hours in Stretton park after a morning of swimming. Ironically, the weather behaved for the "dreaded barbecue"; the Rotary Club of Church Stretton again arriving at Camp and treating everyone to one of its specials. I wasn't a big fan of these events, as readers of my previous books will know. All the same, I was very grateful to the Rotary Club, as we all were.

The following words are those of the Skipper. I have to say right now that I disagree with his final sentence. We had just returned to Camp from Towyn, where the boys had enjoyed a great day at our usual seaside resort:

*Tuesday 1st August:*

*The day was marred by the arrival of the parent of XX. XX had phoned home from Towyn to ask his father to fetch him home.*

*This was a bit of a surprise to say the least because he had been working well in his tent group, and had done very well in sporting activities.*

*Well he was allowed to go home but it does disrupt things, and there is always the danger of an 'epidemic' being started when the lads see one boy going home.*

My reason for disagreeing with Alan's comments about an "epidemic" starting is because I doubt any of the boys would want to go home on the strength of one individual making that decision. Admittedly it wasn't a unique occasion, but it was very rare indeed for one of the lads to ask to be collected prematurely. And why the boy decided to leave us remains one of life's mysteries! I mentioned in one of my earlier books that I myself had taken a lad home. But the reason was entirely different, especially when you read (above) that in this instance the boy had joined in and was doing well.

My disagreement with Alan's final sentence is borne out by Alan himself, by what he wrote in the log on the final day. Sunday 4th August: a "cracking end of Camp looms on the horizon".

It was indeed a cracking end to Camp '96. The afternoon "Scavenger Hunt" went well, and whilst it was going on, Alan and Phil Woods embarked on a wood-collecting mission for the evening Campfire.

Alan notes how difficult it is getting (as we mature in age) to sing all the songs around the Campfire. But with my help, he adds, we succeeded again. The Bosun was in full voice, too, as were most of the lads, and staff, and our guests.

At the end of the evening, after the lads had retired, the Skipper and I sang a few lullabies outside the tents. The occupants were soon asleep!

Monday 5th August. The following words were written by the Camp Skipper, Alan Preece:

*Time to pack up and go! The lads were fairly good in helping to get things moving, and soon were waiting with packed bags for the transport home. They were collected in three batches.*

*It was very gratifying to see the tears roll when they were set for home. I don't think there was a dry eye to be seen. I suppose it is this more than anything during - and after - Camp, that makes you realise that yes, we did get it right.*

*Although we were a bit thin on the ground (for help packing up) we managed to get all the tents down, and bagged up, and clean the site.*

*Many thanks for all the hard work.*

*Alan Preece*

*Skipper 1996.*

I would like to offer now, as I did back then, my sincere thanks to my late friend Alan, and also to my son Marc, for the brilliant job they did. Both agreed to take on a position, the highest offices the Camp had, with very limited prior knowledge of what the job entailed.

Who's who: Camp '96

Tent One: Leader Nicky Piggott. Ricky Gretton, Gary Sutton, Karl Witton, Steve Vaughn, Steven Bebb, Anthony Sutton, Lea O'Connor.

Tent Two: Leader Alan Scriven. Jamie Preece, Paul Bird, Andrew Stephens, Jamie Stephens, John Leith, Mathew Pritchard, Shane Sweeney.

Tent Three: Leader Steve Webb. Lewis Brookes, David Power, Daniel Taylor, Mathew Homer, Philip Pritchard, Warren Teece.

Tent Four: Leader Dave Shaw. James Hickman, Keith Burke,

Wayne Hardy, Neil Lowndes, Nigel Stokes, David Shields, Paul Helps.

Tent Five: Leader Steve Phillips. Richard Harrickie, Stefan Bird, Mark Curtis, Sam Curtis, Chris Cooke, Gary Garavan.

Staff:

Alan Preece (Skipper), Marc Scriven (Bosun), Wendy Smith (Cook/QM), Tom Scriven, Patrick Harte, Annie Williams (Kitchen), Phil Woods (part-time help).

The Skipper's final words on Camp '96:

*My sincere thanks to all the staff for a great job done*

*Special thanks to Alan Scriven for his support and advice, when needed, and for the very professional way in which he accepted his role for this year; and for allowing me to carry on as Skipper in my own style.*

*Thank you also to Marc for an excellent job done as Bosun. I think that anyone who ever doubted his ability to rise to the task can now cast their doubts aside.*

*Some favourite quotes from the boys:*

*'Skipper can we sing "God Save Our Croatian Queen" again' (Sam Curtis)*

*'Can we play Harbour Light again tonight Skip?' (all the lads!)*

*Brilliant; just brilliant!*

# Chapter Thirteen

The Annual General Meeting took place on Tuesday 22nd October 1996 at the Camp premises. It was attended by every member, with the exception of Francis Rudge, who sent his apologies. In actual fact, Francis had not played much of a part in committee business since Bill left. I never harboured any ill feeling for his loyalty to Bill; indeed, if I could have turned the clock back...

Alan Preece did not attend, either, but would have been expected to, in order to submit his “Skipper’s Report”. He was, however, roundly thanked for stepping into the breach, forcibly vacated by yours truly; and for doing a very acceptable job. Marc Scriven was applauded for his success as Bosun, as were the rest of the staff of Camp ’96... including me.

When the annual voting for officers took place, everyone who held office was returned for another year. To my utter surprise, I was also reinstated as Skipper, without a single vote against. When the vote result was announced, I thought immediately of Pat H, and Bill. I know it would have pleased the former; I can only hope it did the latter too, when he received the news... as, without any doubt, he would have done.

I had been very silly in writing that awful letter to Bill, and being stupid enough to write it on a LAC letterhead, too. And I know I’ve said this a million times, but I truly am sorry for the undeniable hurt it caused Bill, and perhaps his family, too. I say perhaps, because I don't know exactly how much they knew about what had happened between us since Bill's association with his much-loved Camp ended. But Annie and Debbie have read my books, and are still my very good friends, and for this I will always be extremely grateful.

I could never hope to equal Bill's love of the wonderful, magical thing he almost single-handedly created, but I don't think anyone other than he could love it more than I did.

An announcement at the AGM by the chair, Barrie Gretton, informed us that talks with the WRVS regarding the possibility of returning to two Camps per year (albeit, each one being just one week long in duration), were imminent. I was happy about this, and hoped we could get a definite agreement. We did, at the party (see below).

The year closed with a first-ever Christmas party being held at Camp. It was attended by thirty-five people, all connected to the Camp, and it was a huge success. The party included the talks with the WRVS mentioned above; the result being two Camps to operate in 1997.

Who could have possibly known or even guessed what was to happen to our beloved Camp, post-1997?

My first book tells in detail of the extraordinary events of 1997: my second walk to Camp to raise funds; the end of the "Cold

War" between Bill and I; the change of format regarding Camp dates, and the break of a near-forty-year tradition on seaside day.

On a staffing note, Dean Nightingale joined up with us again, and I cannot express enough my gratitude to him for what he did for us on the farcical seaside day (told in detail in my first book, on pages 376 and 377).

I kept my eldest son Marc as Bosun, because we were without Alan Preece, and Marc had done a very acceptable job last year as Alan's number two. Alan's omission was down to health reasons; he couldn't possibly have been involved, much as he wanted to be.

It was very strange to be at Camp for set-up day on a Friday, followed by the first-night party on the Saturday, and the boys arriving on the Sunday (27$^{th}$ July). Weird!

We took responsibility for thirty-one boys, ten being lads from Rochdale, and the remainder from Shropshire. No boys from the West Midlands joining us should have immediately raised my concerns... but to be honest, the way it was beginning to pan out should have shown me the writing on the wall anyway!

Nevertheless, the first Camp of 1997 passed into the history books on a satisfactory note, in spite of the weather and periodic poor behaviour.

The boys were collected on Friday 1$^{st}$ August after lunch. Some of the staff left for a weekend at home; I stayed at Camp.

Staff 1997: Alan Scriven (Skipper), Marc Scriven (Bosun), Wendy Smith (QM/Cook).

Tent Leaders: Dean Nightingale; David Shaw; Phil Woods; Tom Scriven; Neil Harrison; Steve Phillips and Nicky Piggott (part-time).

The lads who kindly joined us for Camp 1:

Tent One: Christopher Lee, Luke Kershaw, Michael Gentle, Craig Rhodes, Daniel Hughes, Adam Welch, Sebastian Yapp.

Tent Two: Christopher Thomas, Leon Preston, Phillip O'Brien, Jamie Bagnall, Richard Evans, Lee Smith.

Tent Three: Christopher Bond, Anthony Sweeney, Sean Highfield, Andrew Ashton, Aaron Brine, Carl Owen.

Tent Four: Ricci Gretton, Ian Callaghan (Best Camper), Kyle Teale, Ben Cocker, Daniel Rhodes, Stephan Bird.

Tent Five: Mathew Challinor, Jason Challinor, Dominic Sharkey, Scott Sharkey, Damien Rhodes, Daniel Bagnall.

Some brothers chose to stay together, whilst others separated completely.

Camp Two of 1997 (and, as it turned out, the final Camp ever) began in earnest on Sunday 3rd August. I drove to Wolverhampton to collect members of staff who had decided to spend a day at home. The boys arrived at 12:30hrs; a small group of just twenty-six, the smallest Camp since the very first one in 1959, when twenty-seven lads attended. How ironic is that!

The detail of that final Camp is in my previous books, but I don't mind repeating that the highlight, without doubt, was the long-awaited return of Skipper Bill Williams. It was one of the best days of my life. I invited him to take charge after introducing him as "the real Skipper", and he accepted, with a smile I had not witnessed since Camp 1989.

I then, with Marc's approval (he was just as happy to see our Skipper back as everyone else there who had worked with him pre-1990) fell back into the Bosun's position for the day.

A "first" on the last Camp (the fifty-first, in thirty-nine years) was the date of the ghost hunt. Due to the two Camps being shorter than our usual ten-day affairs, we did the hunt on Monday 4th August. The ghosts were played with due aplomb by Neil Harrison and Phil Woods. The only difference to the evening was a slight change in the actual "ghost story".

The days rolled on far too quickly and soon we were waking up to the penultimate day: Thursday 7th August 1997.

The children had a lie-in ready for the rigorous delights of Sports Day. The weather could not have been any better, which helped everyone to thoroughly enjoy the afternoon.

I spoke from the heart with Bill about my feelings regarding where the Camp was now. I apologised again for the past, and said that I thought the Camp was in danger. We agreed that times had changed from the "halcyon days" we enjoyed back in the 60s, 70s and 80s. Bill appeared to accept what I was saying, which, to be honest, made me feel worse, because the old feelings of guilt began stirring in my head again. But what I said and did in 1989 and 1990 were, in my best judgement at the time, for the greater good of the Longmynd Adventure Camp. You live and learn...!

On Friday 8th August, we bade farewell to the group of lads who had enjoyed a wonderful country holiday at our Camp. It would be the final time we would do so. Meetings and discussions were ahead of me, but no solution would be found to the (in my opinion) unfair demands of the newly appointed WRVS chief of Children's Holidays. I use the term "unfair" intentionally, although admitting that times were changing and therefore changes would have to be made. But all I asked for was a little bit of time. Our ruby anniversary was fast approaching, and Bill Williams was once again on board. I pleaded the case to sanction a group of children to share the historic moment with us. It was massively important to me, if not the rest of my so-called colleagues on the (proving to be useless) committee, that we had a Camp in 1998... just the one would have sufficed. My request was flatly refused. Unfair!

Worst of all, however (as I alluded to earlier), was the uncaring, apathetic and blasé attitude of the Longmynd Adventure Camp committee. All of this is told in graphic detail in my first book. But not, however, my latent suspicions of why this was so! Documents have recently come into my possession (anonymously) that, however you view them, could at least give the impression that the unbelievable behaviour of the committee could have been planned. If it wasn't (and I'm merely suggesting the possibility that it might have been), why did the members stick together, and totally refuse my pleas of alternative assistance to help me get a Camp arranged for our 40th anniversary? Why did they just give in, and let the Camp (as we knew it) go? It doesn't make sense. To me, it's as if there was something they knew, or had at least discussed, without my knowledge. I don't want to come across as paranoid; I'm just asking the question... again: Why did every single member of that committee, whilst all in the same room, decide not to at least give the impression that they wanted to support me? Not one person spoke up in support of me.

Maybe, just maybe, the answers can be found in facsimile copies of a "postal conversation" between a member of our committee and a representative of a Welsh organisation which clearly had its sights set on the facilities of the Longmynd Adventure Camp, and how they might be of benefit to them. As I mentioned earlier, copies of this conversation have now found their way to me, and I have read them with interest. I would not wish to include the letters themselves, as they are neither addressed to, nor written by, me.

In short, it appeared that there was already some kind of informal agreement in place that the Camp should be made available to this organisation and that changes were to be made at their suggestion. These changes would include adjustments to the cabins, to make them suited to use in the colder months; improved security; gender-specific washing and toilet facilities; better kitchen and staffroom facilities, to name but a few. There are also references to the staffing of the Camp, and plans for a number of residential trips for school students. Clearly, there were plans underway to change the nature of the Longmynd Adventure Camp, so that it would no longer be recognisable. Bill Williams' initial idea, and all the hard work and generosity of the voluntary staff over the years, were to be cast aside in favour of a more commercial operation.

What I would like you, reader, to consider is this:

The LAC representative mentions that they spoke to everyone about the letter, which lists the other organisation's comments on ideal alterations to the structure, etc., of the LAC, and also an "idea about staff for your own Camp".

I was never involved in discussions on these suggestions to our committee; that is a categorical fact! So, if such discussions did occur, they were conducted without my knowledge!

Secondly, you have to remember that I wasn't "flavour of the month" with the committee after I was "demoted" in effect for the 1996 Camp. Indeed, on page 360 of my first book, I say that I felt like a leper on Camp '96 whenever any member of the committee showed up, which wasn't often, thankfully!

Fair enough, I was reinstated as Skipper at the post-Camp committee meeting. But maybe this was only because of an error my replacement made during Camp '96, which may have found its way to the ears of the members?

I didn't report it, because it was an "incident" involving the Skipper and a tent leader, after I and most other members of staff had retired; a bit of banter during late evening after the children had retired, which was soon forgotten by both parties on the following day; not, however, by one of the senior staff, who was either on the committee at the time, or very soon to join it. So, although I made the decision not to report it, it doesn't mean that the committee didn't get to know about it. Perhaps, as a result, my "goose was beginning to cook"?

By the dawn of 1998, we were in a sticky situation. The WRVS branches in the West Midlands and Shropshire had all but pulled the plug on its sponsorship agreement. Our only hope of future Camps rested in a vice-like grip by the apparent new policy of its Manchester-based chief.

The committee, in its wisdom, decided on one Camp only, to celebrate our glorious ruby anniversary year. I went along with it; well, Bill was back on board, and had promised to be involved in the Camp's unique milestone, even though he had politely refused Don Rogers' offer of a place on a sub-committee (which never actually got off the ground), formed to organise the big day... which as we all know didn't happen. Disgraceful!

At this point, I would like to refer my readers to my first book. Please read from page 381 to page 390; and in particular, the second paragraph of page 388.

To get to the point, I am utterly convinced that there was

never an intention to hold a Camp for us in 1998, much less a celebration!

The letters, combined with the response from the LAC secretary, seem (to me at least) to bear this out. Their required dates for 1998 would have absolutely collided with the dates when we would have held our Camp, although it is fair to say the committee did condescend to agree to me having the weekend of 20th July at Camp with my former members of staff, to say thank you for all their help and support over the preceding years. Our Camps usually began on the following weekend, however. As a matter of interest, and my first book bears this out, I wrote to the committee members, inviting them to come along to Camp (just for a brief visit) to thank the voluntary staff themselves for everything they had done to help get the Camp to the good position it was now in. But not one of them had the decency or courtesy to show their face.

That said, however, no wonder I had received no support whatsoever when I informed the members, my fellow colleagues, earlier of my WRVS meeting.

The call to go to Manchester came out of the blue, as did the tough and uncompromising conditions; and the mention of my intended Camp programme! No ghost hunting and no Harbour Light, because they didn't want anyone off the Campsite after dark! It would have become an adventure camp in name only if I (not we) had managed to get agreement for just that one historic Camp. But better that than nothing!

I can't help thinking now, based on everything that happened in 1998; together with the correspondence from 1996 coming into my possession so unexpectedly, and so late in this sad story, that I, and the Longmynd Adventure Camp as was, were betrayed. The committee meeting I called after my meeting was, in my eyes now, the "Last Supper". And Judas was in that room, with all of his treacherous friends!!

I might add, incidentally, that almost all of the suggested changes (to the Camp premises) were implemented over time. But of course, this may have been simply co-incidental...

I know this from actually spending a few days at the Camp (with some members from our Minton Memories group) in October 2018, when the current committee allowed us to be there to celebrate the Camp's sixtieth anniversary. Needless to say, although an invitation for them to join us was offered, not one single person (and at least one of them was a committee member during my time as a member) accepted.

There was a note left in the hall, from Holyhead School, Birmingham:

*Sunday 24th - Friday 29th June 2018*

*What can we say!*

*Another fantastic D of E Bronze*

*Brilliant Campsite, fantastic facilities - We just love it.*

*Massive thank you to all who help at Longmynd Adventure Camp*

*Holyhead love you.*

Ah... how lovely!! And on the reverse:

*Southall School*

*Malcolm Webster (RIP) was linked to our school; and was a really good friend. His legacy carries on with every visit and every smiling child.*

Now there's a message I can actually agree with. God bless you, Mal.

We thought maybe the committee was holding its own celebrations of the Camp's outstanding achievement... er, no. They didn't even realise, until Annie Williams (Bill's daughter) mentioned it when enquiring as to whether we could hire the site.

Final Camp (1997) Personnel:

Staff: Bill Williams and Alan Scriven (Skippers), Marc Scriven and Alan Scriven (Bosuns), Wendy Smith (QM), Wendy Smith and Dean Nightingale (Cooks),

Tent Leaders: Tony Hammon (1); Neil Harrison (2); Phil Woods (3); Steve Phillips and Tom Scriven (4); Nicky Piggott (part-time)

The lads who made up this final, original format, Camp:

Tent One: Adrian Millman, Damian Sharples, Kris King, Gary (ladd) Bull, William Aston, Ashley Owen.

Tent Two: Mark Whitehurst, Paul Grocott, Chris Grocott, Will

Whitehurst, Mathew Pritchard, Craig Heselwood.

Tent Three: Carl Clutton, Andrew Bagnall, Andrew Locke, Craig Kershaw, Liam Davies, John Luker.

Tent Four: Jamie Penn, Lloyd Brackenbury, Philip Pritchard (Best Camper), Nythan Hadley, Johnathan Hurn, Jordan Gardener, Warren Teece.

# Chapter Fourteen

For the vast majority of the Camp's existence, the Camps were held in close proximity to a valley called Minton Batch. Therefore "the batch", as we fondly referred to it, became a constant throughout the life of the Camp... as we knew it. And we became firm friends with the Davies (hill farming) family, brothers Clifford and Ned, father of the current farmer, Dave. I'm very happy to say that Dave remains to this day a good friend of mine and John Preece, and our friends from our group Minton Memories who join us whenever we Camp on Dave's land in the batch, or hold our monthly meetings.

The older ones amongst, us i.e. John, Mick Powell, Scottie Gibbons and me, have known Dave since our childhood days, when he would regularly be on Camp with us joining in our games. I've mentioned this before; it was Ned and Clifford Davies who sold the land that the Longmynd Adventure Camp stands on today, to Bill Williams and the committee. I thought it would be nice to include some historic details about the batch and one or two Camp stories from across the years. But first, a quote from the late great Mr Bill Williams BEM from 1997 (to a group of lads at Camp):

"In my experience of the Shropshire hills, east and west of the A49, there is no finer place to walk, hike, or just to simply sit and take in the glorious views which are beautiful whatever the season, than the Long Mynd. And Minton Batch, with its busy, winding brook, is one of the very best valley walks in all of the many square miles that make up this fascinating landscape."

Bang on, Skipper!

The Long Mynd is, I think, first mentioned in 1175. The name means "long hill", or "long mountain", which, I believe, is a mix of sorts from the old English "lang", and the Welsh "mynnd".

Viewed from the east, one can clearly see the many hills which combine or morph to make this very attractive part of the region, whereas from the west the view is definitely that of one long hill, a bit like a massive blue whale, atop of which sits the Glider Club.

The Long Mynd is an important and vital part of the Shropshire Hills Area of Outstanding Beauty, of which the National Trust owns approximately half.

Minton Batch is situated a little south of Church Stretton, nestling between the hamlets of Minton and Hamperley (as does the Camp). Both are mentioned in the Domesday Book. Church Stretton, this small but attractive town, was (it is said) given its name by the Romans. It means "Settlement by the Street" (meaning, I suppose, Watling Street, which runs north/south near the eastern edge of the town).

The small valleys off Minton Batch are called Rams Batch (to the right), Hens Batch on the left, immediately after the farm, and Windy Batch, which lies opposite the start of the forestry area. This valley forms part of the area where we played the children's all-time favourite game, Harbour Light.

Whilst in the process of research for this book, I learned that the brook which winds its gentle course through Minton Batch forms (or did at one time) the boundary between the civil parishes of Myndtown and Church Stretton. And apparently, a "holy well" was once situated either at the junction of the batch and the old lane, or in the first field to the right as one enters the valley.

Further into the valley, past the farm, stands a small stone pillar of sorts. It is engraved with the letters "I.J.", and it is in line with the edge of the forestry, standing almost in the brook! Exactly what the letters refer to, I have yet to discover. During my thirty-three years with the Camp I heard, and indeed offered, some interesting and outrageous suggestions: "It's the initials of the bloke who killed the mad axe-man"; "It's the initials of the man who redirected the course of the brook"; "It stands as a tribute to the man who planted the forestry"; "It's a grave." And so on!

Finally, legend has it that a motte-and-bailey castle once stood in Minton Batch... was it anywhere near the "ghost bridge"? I wonder!

Over the years, the batch and the brook have featured largely in the everyday life of most of the souls who were lucky enough to be a part of the Camp. I myself won a contest for holding my breath underwater for the longest time, way back in the sixties.

The brook was dammed up almost every single year so that the lads could play in it. In the part of the brook which ran through the bottom of our field a "greasy pole" was situated across the deepest part (we dammed this part up too) of it, and we used to have pillow fights on the pole to see who could straddle it for the longest time. Brilliant fun; Scottie Gibbons was very good at this!

The one Camp activity which the brook will always be remembered for, however, is the morning washing ritual. Except on very wet mornings when the rain was lashing down on us, we all made the short trek to the clear waters of Minton's brook to have our first wash of the day. Naturally, many of the lads; and, it has to be said, a small number of the staff, dreaded the brook. In the early years, when our Camp enjoyed life on Jack Williams' beautiful piece of Shropshire heaven, it was just a few steps from the tent area, so there would usually be a member of staff (Francis Rudge on most occasions) posted down at the water's edge, to ensure everyone, man and boy, had a thoroughly good wash, to his standards! Ironically, no one ever saw Mr Rudge washing in the brook... he was probably too early for us!

And when the Camp was relocated to its very own bit of land, our walks to the brook and back took some considerable time; very often, the cook would be jumping about in vexed mood because the food was cooling.

As well as the games I've mentioned above, we played lots more in the batch, like Cowboys and Indians, and stalking each other in the high bracken (or fern as it is also called) to the right of the brook.

Minton Batch is one route to the Glider Club on the Long Mynd. One only has to walk to the very end of it; then climb the hill... easier said than done!

Minton Batch was the scene of the worst accident (mentioned earlier) ever to happen off the campsite, and it was also the place where tragedy occurred on a quiet afternoon in the late sixties (I tell the story, which incidentally won me first prize in the *Camp Magazine* contest in 1968, in my first book).

The first bridge in the batch, which obviously served back in the day as a crossing point for the farmers and sheep maybe (too narrow for cattle) was the site of many a concert featuring the "infamous" Minton Moguls, a countryside "super group" which readers of my previous books will be well acquainted with.

In my very early years at Camp, which my friends (and Minton Memories members) John and Keith Preece, Ian 'Scottie' Gibbons, Mick Powell and Len Badger shared with me, there was an old cart just standing there at the top end of the valley. Well, that cart is still there to this very day, albeit in a very sorry and mangled state. I wonder if Scottie and Len remember it; John and Mick would have seen it in its present state quite recently. It just begs the question: Why?

Why was it (seemingly) just abandoned where it lies these days, as no more than a pathetic wreck? It is a very old, almost ancient, piece of farming kit, which I reckon would have cost more than a pretty penny when it was originally acquired by whoever decided to dump it at the end of its "working life".

As I said above, I and a few close friends still camp in the batch, courtesy of hill farmer (and friend) Dave Davies. And apart from the field (just across the lane) where our dreams were made in the sixties and seventies, we wouldn't wish to be anywhere else. Just to emphasise this point, in 2018 John Preece wrote the following, as a tongue-in-cheek tribute to our gratitude to Dave for his continual kindness in allowing us to be there whenever we wish:

*My life it seems in turmoil, whichever way I turn*
*My money just gets eaten up, no matter what I earn.*
*The mortgage, food and utility bills, they always seem to grow*
*And how I'm going to pay them, I just don't seem to know.*
*The house is cold, the food's all gone, and the weather's wet and damp*
*So I'll pack my bags; jump in the car*
*And drive straight back to Camp!*

This final book on the Longmynd Adventure Camp would not be complete without a few words about Church Stretton, as it was the major town (for us), as opposed to Craven Arms. The lads did any shopping they needed to do (presents if the money hadn't dried up), and made use, whenever possible, of the school swimming pool. The park was also frequented by groups who wanted a bit of space and privacy to act out their plays/skits for the Campfire. And in the very early years, the tent leaders would often frequent the local hostelries (usually the Buck's Head, the Vaults, and the King's Arms) if and when they were given a free evening. I can remember only once going into Stretton on my evenings off during the seventies; it was too much of a walk... to and from!

Skipper would never allow us to drive, so pretty soon we all made the Ragleth and the Green Dragon pubs in Little Stretton our locals, before we ceased going out altogether, when the Skipper obtained a temporary alcohol licence for the duration of the Camp(s). The partaking in an alcoholic beverage was controlled firmly by the boss. No drinking during the day (except for one drink only at Sunday lunch) and only a couple in the evening, after the children had retired, if you were not on field duty.

Church Stretton's "story" starts in the far geological past, according to the large information boards in Easthope Road. A massive earthquake caused the Church Stretton Fault.

All through the prehistoric age, people tended to live mainly in the hills. Then later, Bronze Age farmers cleared the trees from the hills; and by the time of the Iron Age, hill forts were home to large numbers of sheep and cattle belonging apparently to the Cornovi tribe.

After their invasion of Britain, the Romans built a major road for military purposes through the Stretton Gap, from Chester to South Wales, via Wroxeter. But although they were so close (at Wroxeter), the Romans didn't have very much influence on Stretton. When the Romans eventually left, Saxon farmers settled close to the road.

Not long after the Norman Conquest, the Earl of Shrewsbury took control. The Normans erected an earth and timber motte-and-bailey castle on Castle Hill in All Stretton. They also rebuilt the wooden Saxon church, later dedicated to St Laurence.

The Normans were very clever! Early in the twelfth century, they soon realised that the way to calm the volatile borderlands was to grant, by royal command, the right to hold a weekly market... and an annual fair. So added to this were the large profits from manorial and monastic flocks of sheep, which ensured the town's prosperity. The real important asset was, however, its ideal location, on the Shrewsbury-Hereford border. And in an effort to quell Welsh marauders, the locals were offered a shilling for every Welsh head! One claimed 57 shillings!

By 1327, Stretton had a population of approximately 150 people, living in just thirty-eight households, all paying taxes.

In 1337, King Edward III granted Church Stretton a charter for a weekly market on Thursdays, so the grant by the Normans was compounded!

In the 1360s, the population was all but decimated by the infamous Black Death.

We jump to the sixteenth century, and in the first half of it; in fact, as early as 1509, perhaps the most famous of all British monarchs, Henry VIII, succeeded his father, Henry VII, who had most fortuitously grabbed the crown at the battle of Bosworth from King Richard III in 1485. His claim to the throne was at best extremely slight and Richard was well prepared (or so he thought) when Henry Tudor landed from France to challenge the King. Henry's supporters joined him as he made his way from Pembrokeshire to Leicester via Shrewsbury, but he was vastly outnumbered by the King's army. When battle eventually commenced, Richard soon gained the upper hand. Unfortunately, however, having seized his opportunity to confront and kill Henry, he was betrayed by the Stanleys, who joined forces with Henry. Richard rode straight into a well-laid trap and was unhorsed and unprotected. He was killed instantly by a blow from (it is widely accepted) Rhys ap Thomas, who in fact was a traitor. He had previously sworn allegiance to Richard; even stating that Henry Tudor would land in Wales "over my belly". After this betrayal, he was knighted by Henry VII.

So, as a result of Henry VIII's fall-out with the Bishop of Rome, the King desecrated all the monasteries loyal to Rome. And beautiful Shropshire didn't escape Henry's wrath! The monasteries' estates were sold off to the local gentry, and when the new landowners tried to enclose traditional sheep walks on the Long Mynd and hills of Stretton, they were seen off by angry commoners; good on 'em, I say!

The Great Fire of 1593 destroyed almost all of Church Stretton's tightly-packed timber-frame buildings. In fact, the only buildings to survive the fire were the church, and the Buck's Head Inn.

Between 1642 and 1651, the passing soldiery disrupted lots of Shropshire's towns, and communities.

As the Industrial Revolution arrived, Parliament attempted to introduce tolls to pay for main road improvements, but this angered the farmers and drovers. So later, when the Enclosures Act of 1890 came in, the Long Mynd was exempted, due to the ancient manorial commoners' rights. Progress, however, continued, with the structure of Stretton's first water-powered mill - Carding Mill - between 1812 and 1824.

The 1831 census returns recorded 1302 inhabitants in the parish.

In the Victorian era, the new railway line between Shrewsbury and Ludlow opened in 1852, with a station at Church Stretton, bringing slow change; steam trains brought grain for the local malthouses, and carried away local farm produce. And the Church Stretton Hotel (later "The Hotel") opened in 1865, serving teas, etc.

The population had risen to almost 1,700, according to the 1861 census.

1866 saw the completion of Town Brook Hollow reservoir, still there to this day. The reservoir supplied all of the town's water. Mick Powell, my son Marc and I regularly pass it on our frequent

Pole Bank walks. And in 1880 the Men's Club, as it is known, and Reading Room were established.

It came as something of a surprise (if not a shock) to me to learn that from 1881 local Church Stretton water was bottled and exported by the Stretton Hills Mineral Water Co.

In 1884, the Rev. Holland Sandford started planting lime trees on what was then Station Road. As a result, the road became Sandford Avenue.

Church Stretton and its surrounding areas have a very interesting history. From 1895, some Bronze Age barrows on the Long Mynd were converted into grouse-shooting butts. And the late 1800s heralded new roads, built by the local land company, either side of the valley, to cater for housing, etc. Also, a nine-hole golf course - one of the highest in England (and later extended to eighteen holes) - was laid out on the Mynd.

During the final year of the nineteenth century, Church Stretton Urban District Council was formed. Also, the poet A.E. Housman (he who immortalised south Shropshire as "the land of the lost continent" and "those blue remembered hills") was a guest of the town on three occasions.

From c.1900, local inns which provided accommodation included the Buck's Head, the Raven, and the King's Arms. All three are still very much in business today, too.

The town continued to progress through the early years of the new century. The 1901 census recorded a population of 1,749. A local author, Mary Webb, honeymooned in Stretton. And in her novels the town was called “Shepwardine”. In the same year that the First World War started (in which fifty local men died), a new railway station was opened on the south side of Sandford Avenue bridge. Towards the end of the war, the Silvester Horne Institute opened.

Just a couple of years later, Church Stretton became a tourist attraction as day-trippers arriving by charabanc flocked to the town... and Carding Mill Valley.

The 1921 census tells us that the population had grown again. There were now 2,650 inhabitants in the parish. The Midlands Gliding Club was established in 1934, and three years later the Regal Cinema opened its doors in Sandford Avenue. A supermarket stands on the spot these days.

The Second World War came and went, with a loss of life to the town amounting to thirty-one servicemen and women. It was during the war (from 1940) that St Dunstan’s charity for the blind evacuated to Church Stretton from the dangerous South Coast. Another effect of the war was the number of British and American planes that crashed on the Long Mynd during training sessions.

In 1941, two women were killed by snowdrifts on the Long Mynd.

Seven years into the reign of Queen Elizabeth II, Rectory Field (and the wood) was purchased by the County Council as a public open space. Mick Powell, my son Marc and I walk regularly through Rectory Wood on our way to Carding Mill Valley, via the highest point on the Long Mynd: Pole Bank. The Long Mynd and the Stretton hills have been hiked over many times by us, and my youngest son Tom, during and since our time with the Camp. My grandson Connor has expressed a wish to join us on our long walks, too, and I can't wait for him to become one of our number!

Early in 2020, we took part in a sponsored walk to raise funds for a lasting memorial to Bill Williams BEM. It proved to be a fantastic day out for all regular members of our Minton Memories group, who either walked or met us at Pole Cottage, to spur us on with snacks and a sing-song. I would like to thank them all, and also the kind people who got sponsorship and joined us on the walk: Tony and Shirley Brunyee (workmates of mine); Richard and Angela Hough, and their daughter Hollie (long-time friends of our family); Darren Stones (workmate) and his partner Debbie. There would have been more of us, but I had to postpone the walk at least a couple of times, which altered some potential walkers' plans. We still managed to considerably add to the fund, though, and that's the main thing!

In 1960, the new secondary school opened on the Shrewsbury Road, and eight years later St Laurence C of E Primary School opened (also on Shrewsbury Road). Ten years after this, in 1978, the National Trust acquired Carding Mill Valley, the Batch (not Minton Batch), and Bodbury Hill.

More progress regarding business and housing saw the local population rise to 4,184 in 1991, which was an increase of 1,514 from 1958, according to the Church Stretton Guidebook.

I was awarded the MBE in 2001 for "Thirty Years Voluntary Service to Disadvantaged Young People" (citation). On a more negative note, however, 2001 saw Foot and Mouth disease raise its ugly head on parts of the Long Mynd, which adversely affected businesses in the area. Also in that year, Church Stretton Parish Council voted to become a Town Council, thus creating the post of Town Mayor.

Towards the back end of the first decade of the new millennium, Church Stretton was the first town in the Midlands to be awarded the prestigious "Walkers are Welcome" status.

And to close this brief historic look at the beautiful town between the villages of Little Stretton and All Stretton, in 2010 a new sports and leisure centre opened for business at Church Stretton School.

Today it's all about tourism (which has now replaced agriculture as the mainstay of the town's economy); and an ageing population!

# Chapter Fifteen

My Camp logbook records the following, written by me in December 1997, when it wasn't completely obvious that the Camp was in fact dead in the water:

*Since the end of the 1997 Camps, I have received a nice letter from Wendy Smith (Rochdale WRVS). Hopefully, we will have her input and support for next year.*

*I have met with Bill Williams on a couple of occasions, and he has kindly given me some documents/material relating to the earlier Camps, which will greatly assist me in my effort to write the history of the Camp.*

*As well, I have met our Chair Barrie Gretton a few times, and I get the feeling we have different views on the future of the Camp. I will not compromise my ideas and intentions for the Camp, going forward, should I be re-elected as Skipper at the AGM.*

*I cannot and will not allow the committee to tell me who I can and cannot have as members of staff whilst the Camp is operative; this has ALWAYS been the sole decision of the Camp leadership, and the committee have absolutely no right to question that!*

*Barrie has threatened to resign his position if I insist on having anyone on Camp who he thinks I should not. I will resign if he or any other member of the committee (of which we have both been members since July 1st 1981) is allowed to have any input into what is essentially a CAMP MATTER, not committee business. The AGM is arranged for 03 December 1997.*

February 1998 logbook entry:

*Well at last the disagreement (mentioned above) has been cleared up, and everyone is happy.*

*We will have just the one Camp this year, reverting to a "ten-dayer". As things stand at this moment however, we don't yet know from where the children will be coming from (WRVS region) for this Camp, our fifty-second, which falls in our Ruby (40yrs) anniversary year. I can't wait!*

The fact is, however, I am still waiting... and will do so forever!!!

I said in my logbook entry for December 1997 that resignations would be a result if Barrie or I got "our way" regarding him wanting committee input in Camp staffing positions. And then in my entry of February 1998 I write that the problem had been solved amicably. I can't help wondering now, and I am in no way "pointing the finger", if that may have been a reason why the committee gave me no support whatsoever after I appraised all members of my disastrous meeting in Manchester.

To put it bluntly, as I have suggested above, this might have been their strategy: *If we don't support him on this, he will probably resign.*

Well, it's certainly a possibility; I was always known for sticking to my guns. And when I did resign a little while after realising that no help from the either WRVS management or the committee was forthcoming, the possibility of another person to operate the Camps (according to the committee's instructions and decisions, seemingly) was announced. That failed to come to fruition, however, due to reasons involving the person who was to take my place, apparently.

The result was that no holiday Camps (operated in its original format) have been held since the second Camp of 1997. And that is (in my opinion) a travesty beyond words!

The LAC does, however, profess to still cater for the type of child Bill Williams created it for, according to its spasmodic publications. We also have to consider the "ideas for staffing your Camps" mentioned in the correspondence I have recently acquired, in the light of my fall-out with Barrie about the very subject... in 1997.

I promised at the beginning of this third and absolutely final book on the history of the first forty years of the Longmynd Adventure Camp that I would include towards the end a special poem written by my good friend, and fellow Camp staff member, the writer and playwright Owen J. Lewis (you'll find him on Facebook as Owen "Scribbler" Lewis). If you have read my previous books, as well as this one (thank you); or if you are a former beneficiary of the Camp, or a voluntary member of staff, his words will resonate with you. Here it is; I hope you enjoy it:

***Those were the Days!***

*I walked the sharp steep valley, along through Minton Batch,*
*The time was middle summer when all the small birds hatch.*
*I heard far in the distance, a laugh; a cry and a call,*
*So I slowly sat and listened, in fear that I might fall.*
*But I'd listened back in history; I heard a time now gone,*
*And I heard the young boys' laughter, and I thought of everyone.*
*This was the very valley, the backdrop to the scene,*
*The start to all adventures now calm, and quiet, and green.*
*For fifty years the lads had come to play upon this land,*
*All of it made possible by one man's steady hand.*
*One man and his helpers appeared here year on year,*
*To a Camp he made for youngsters, who knew little more than fear.*
*He made for them a holiday; somewhere that they could play,*
*Way off in the distant hills we made their summer's day.*
*We explored with them together the nature, rocks, and breeze,*
*We showed them how to spot a bird, or identify the trees.*

*We gave them love and nurture; they gave to us such fun,*
*A two-way street of merriment, that touched us; everyone.*
*As I sit, the water gushes, on its bed of ancient stone,*
*And I close my eyes, remembering, and then I'm not alone.*
*Although the children no more come, their spirit fills these hills,*
*I remember all their laughter, their dreams and all the thrills.*
*I think of the friends I made back then, and all of the times that passed,*
*And now I hold them in my heart, and will do until the last.*
*But all of this was possible, those happy hours we spent,*
*Because one great man came along,*
*With his heart; a dream... and a tent!*

By Owen J. Lewis (April 2020)

I sincerely hope that I've taken my readers on an interesting journey through the first forty years of a fantastic place which I and so many others were so fortunate to be a small part of. When I saw for the first time, at the tender age of twelve years, the field that was to be my home for ten days, I was filled with horror and dread! I had only once before left my home for any length of time, and that was for a few days at the seaside with the school. This new place meant sleeping in a tent which couldn't be properly secured at night. Therefore, in my mind, I was vulnerable to all the wild beasts that wandered about in the deep countryside looking, nay hunting, for food! It didn't matter that my brother Billy had been to this place a year before, and loved every minute of it. No, I was scared stiff... for a couple of days!

Then the big copper, his merry men (Mick Powell the merriest, he was always happy, and brilliant fun), the lady cook Mrs Hull, and my fellow Campers all came together to give me, Scottie Gibbons, Len Badger, John Preece, and a host of others, a free holiday we would never forget!

People I will always remember fondly, some now lost to us, became good friends, even if it was only for the time we spent together at this beautiful paradise we had been led to by our fairy godmother, Mrs Marjorie Lathe of Wolverhampton WVS. Other boys from many towns/cities up and down the country had their fairy godmother, too. Good, dedicated, salt-of-the-earth ladies, some of whom I had the privilege to meet and work with during the years I was a part of the Camp's senior staff, including Kim Harris and Mrs Roscoe (Shropshire); Daisy Stephens (Dudley); Wendy Smith (Rochdale), and Diane Hogg (Wolverhampton). These ladies selected the lads (some year on year, like me and my brothers) who they considered would benefit from ten days in the idyllic South Shropshire countryside, and made sure each one of us had everything we needed to be comfortable, i.e. clothing, baggage, and even spending money. I'm sure I speak for every single young lad who ever set foot on those hallowed fields between 1958 and 1997, when I say, sincerely: Thank you all, ladies, very much indeed; a diamond, every one!

What a pity, then, that no one could (or perhaps it was more they didn't want to) slow the changing times, policies and attitudes of those who held sway on Children's Holidays at the close of the twentieth century.

Below is a poem I wrote following the passing of the great man who influenced my life more than any other.
My dear friend, Bill:

*And now you've gone, there's a void in my life which encompasses all of my fears.*
*I beg your forgiveness for my lack of understanding; I'm so sorry for the long, lost years.*
*But please don't give up on me now that we're friends again,*
*Stay with me, walk again with me; be with me always.*
*I'll see you in the sunshine of every fresh new dawn, and in each and every raindrop of every summer storm.*
*I'll see you in the millions of stars that shine down from heaven bright.*
*I'll see you in the rivers as they travel to the sea,*
*And I'll hear your voice in the music that softens life for me.*
*I'll see you in every autumn leaf that turns from green to gold,*
*And in the falling winter snow that makes the days so cold.*
*I'll think of you, my friend and mentor each day, more and more;*
*I wish you love, light and peace as you go through the brightest door.*
*And as a veil of sadness falls around everything we had,*
*I'll remember all the good times at Camp; that won't ever make me sad.*

Bill Williams was a special kind of man; a man who oozed compassion but never buckled when he had an opinion. He was a much-respected man who put others first, at all times. He was a fun-loving man, who could take a joke, and also commit a prank on his friends. His police career stretched across twenty-five years, during which time he served as Chair of the Police Federation, representing all ranks below Superintendent.

Bill Williams was indeed a legend in his own lifetime, and I for one am a better person for sharing a small part of his fascinating life.

So, after telling the no-holds-barred history of the first forty years of the Longmynd Adventure Camp, and what was happening in my life during this period of time, we arrive at the final words:

From the thousands of young lads whose lives you enhanced; the many persons who felt privileged to give their time completely free, to help make the Camp the success it undoubtedly was; the scores of people whose lives you touched by way of your Camp, and the countless others whose lives were blessed from knowing you, either as a member of the family, friend or simply an acquaintance, we say as one:

Thank you very much, Skipper, for all our memories.

As I mentioned, I formed a group chat on Facebook called "LAC Sixty Years" in 2017, after the publication of my first book. I was delighted to be contacted via social media, by some long-forgotten former Camp staff members, and also some of the people who had been boys on Camp at the same time as me. The first to be invited to join were Bill's daughters Ann and Debbie... and it just grew!

The fundamental reason for forming the group was to set the record straight, so to speak, regarding the lack of any sort of recognition by the LAC's current committee for the Camp's Diamond Anniversary. Actually, I doubt very much whether most of its members even knew the charity had reached this historic moment.

We all agreed that we should do something. Various suggestions were put forward, and we decided on the following:

Ann Lewis (née Williams) would make initial contact with the committee member responsible for letting the Camp premises. She would explain about our group, and say that we would like to hire the Camp (at their convenience), in order to hold our own celebration of the Camp's sixtieth anniversary... unless they were doing something similar?

No; they had nothing planned, was the response. The first date available, however, was the end of October 2018. Ann accepted and there would be no charge. Very gracious of Mr Dawson, and we all appreciated it.

The group members who were actively involved at that point were the following:

Annie Williams

Debbie Bridge (née Williams)

Ian Gibbons (former beneficiary, and staff member 1960s/1970s)

Carol Gibbons (Ian's wife)

Kim Harris (former WRVS Shrewsbury 1990s)

Gordon Harris (husband of Kim, and part-time staff member 1992)

Mick Powell (former staff member 1960s/1970s)

Diana Powell (wife of Mick)

Owen Lewis (former staff member 1980s/1990s)

Lee Knowles (friend of Owen)

Kevin Duggins (former staff member 1980s/1990s)

Marc Scriven (former jnr + snr staff member 1980s/1990s, at Camp since 1979)

Dean Nightingale (beneficiary 1980s; staff member 1980s/1990s)

John Preece (former beneficiary1960s: staff member 1980s/1990s)

Pete Roberts (former staff member 1960s/1970s)

Not all those mentioned above actually took advantage of the committee's offer, but most of them did visit regularly. It was a very cold few days, but we all loved being back at our “spiritual home”. We had informed the local press (*Shropshire Star* and *Chronicle*) of our intention to be at Camp to celebrate its Diamond Anniversary. The idea was to put the word out; inviting everyone who had ever been a part of the Camp in whatever capacity to come along and share one special day with us all. I envisaged lots of people whom I/we hadn’t seen for years, or had perhaps never even met, to come and share their own memories of Camp. Mick Powell and Ian Gibbons did a fantastic job of decorating the whole front of the site. I took along all my memorabilia and photographs, which I set out on a few tables. John Preece again proved what an excellent cook he is. We all donated raffle prizes, the cash from which would go into a fund to pay for our next project (more on this below), for Bill’s work to be honoured properly. We thought (foolishly, as it transpired) that maybe the committee or at least some of its more senior members would come and join the momentous occasion of the Camp’s sixtieth anniversary.

As it turned out, no one outside our “Camp family”, which included Stephen Phillips (staff member 1990s) and Keith Preece (beneficiary 1960s/staff member 1980s) bothered to join us. There were plenty of promises, but every single one broken for whatever reason (perhaps the weather was the stand-out one). Still, as I said above, we enjoyed it; we loved it, actually, and resolved to do it again the following year during summertime, if permission could again be granted (sad to say we needed permission after the years we had worked on, and looked after the site). The site is a going concern for most of the year, I concede; hence permission being required.

Whilst at Camp, it dawned on us that no memorial had been instigated by the current committee, in honour of the passing of the Camp's founder, Chair and Skipper from 1959 to 1989. Yes, a large framed drawing of Bill (kindly given by the family) hung on one of the walls in the main hall, but no indication of the man's achievements accompanied it. In fact, there is little to no formal recognition of any part of the Camp's glorious history.

To me, it beggars belief (with no disrespect to the late Barrie Gretton) that they honoured the person who took Bill's place as chair of the committee in 1990 (after Bill left) with a memorial bench, complete with plaque, which stands right outside the doors of the hall; no one could miss it! I have no problem with Barrie's memorial. But at no time during the intervening years did any one of the committee, apparently, even suggest that similar respect ought to be afforded to the man who started it all... from scratch!

I was determined to put that right! Firstly, I changed our group name to Minton Memories.

During our few days at Camp in October 2018, Stephen Phillips made a beautiful leather-bound memorial book with loose leaf pages for anyone that wanted to leave a message about being back at Camp; their memories of it, or thoughts regarding our reasons for being there. I have carefully stored the pages of comments in my Camp records files (available for anyone to view whenever the opportunity arises), but I think it might be an idea to share some of them here.

The words are exactly as they were scribed:

*30th October 2018*

*My sincere thanks to everyone who kindly came to support us during our celebrations for the Camp's 60th anniversary*

*We, the people who were a part - in whatever capacity - during 1958 and 1998 have enjoyed our time here this week.*

*I am eternally grateful to the late Mr Bill Williams BEM, for making it all possible. God bless you Sir.*

*Alan Scriven (Camp beneficiary; staff member 1965 - 1998.)*

*30th October 2018*

*I came "I saw"; didn't see many. But it was the ones I did see that mattered!!!*

*(They know who they are)*

*We will all be together one day.*

*God bless*

*D A Nightingale (LAC 1983/1997)*

*I was one of the 60's boys. There are no words to express my feelings regarding the start in life the Camp gave me.*

*My thanks go to Bill "Skip" Williams for all he did, and the sterling work that Alan did, in following in his footsteps.*

*"Each of us leaves footprints in the sand. None of us know how long before the sea washes them away".*

*Live life to the full*

*Ian "Scottie" Gibbons*

*I was a member of Wistanstow Youth Club. I was in my late teens when Bill asked if I would like to join him and others at a Boys Camp in Minton. I became a tent leader, taking charge of tent no.2. I got on well with everyone, and helped, as they did to make this most important Camp to succeed, which it did!*

*We are here to honour the founder, Mr Bill Williams BEM, who started it 60 years ago. It has brought a few tears, meeting up with so many friends from the past. I have missed the Camp and the people from it.*

*Mick Powell*

*Happy 60th Anniversary LAC*

*Bill Williams recognised that children only get one childhood. The Longmynd Adventure Camp has helped so many children to have a memorable one. Thank you.*

*With love and fond memories from Kim (WRVS) and Gordon Harris*

# Chapter Sixteen

It probably was the cold weather that kept many people from joining us to celebrate, in our own simple way, the Camp's sixtieth year. But we considered the weekend a success ourselves, and shortly afterwards the main members of our group met up again at the Ragleth pub to consider another project to honour our (the LAC's) founder, and his magnanimous work over four decades.

We decided on a memorial bench; not because we wanted to match the one that had been placed on the Camp in honour of the late Barrie Gretton, we simply thought it would be a fitting tribute.

The bench was supplied by Bill's youngest daughter, Debbie, while her older sister daughter Annie covered the cost of the two plaques, and I paid for the photograph to be positioned between them. All that was left to do was arrange a date convenient to the LAC committee, and plan the day's programme.

Again, the committee were generous in allowing us to use the Camp facilities at no cost. But, despite another invitation, this time to join us for the bench "unveiling ceremony", no one accepted! No great surprise.

The ceremony was scheduled for Saturday 29th June 2019,

although most of the group spent the actual weekend at Camp, and this time the weather was brilliant; warm days and sunshine throughout! And on this momentous occasion, our numbers swelled appreciatively, which was brilliant. We invited former Bishop Richard Lewis to perform the unveiling ceremony, with Ann and Debbie sitting either end of the bench. Richard is a valued friend of the Williams family from their Wistanstow years, and a former tent leader from my time at Camp as a boy. He was the ideal choice, and he performed his "duty" perfectly. It was a truly fantastic and memorable day, and I would like to offer my sincere thanks to Richard, and everyone else who came to take part!

Earlier, a group of us "old boys": Scottie Gibbons, Len and Edwin Badger, Charlie Gunter and I, joined Scottie's former tent leader Mick Powell on a "nostalgic walk" to the field where we had lots of memories. For Charlie, however, his memories were encased in Endeavour Cottage, where he had enjoyed his time with Bill and his fellow Campers back in 1961.

Amongst the "legends" that joined us on the 29th were: Kevin Duggins, Marc Scriven, Nicola Piggott, and Chris Toolan (former police colleague of Bill's, and Camp staff 1960s/70s).

Pete Roberts (another police colleague) sadly didn't make the day, due to his father's ongoing health problems, but sent his best wishes. Pete, who was actually my tent leader in 1968, features in my second book; telling in his own words how he came to join Bill's staff list.

After a relaxed morning, invited guests began to arrive at Camp; it soon felt like we had never been away from it; and each other... if only!

Our visitors included Lyn Williams and her sister Maria (the daughters of former Camp staff members Don and Eileen Mansell of Church Stretton). They both enjoyed their day and had a really good time.

The bench was covered with a large Union flag and, when the time came for Richard to unveil it, we all gathered round. Before the actual unveiling, he gave a short talk; explaining who he was, when he was at Camp, and how honoured he felt to be asked “out of everyone you could have chosen” to perform this “great and extremely worthwhile deed”.

It was our pleasure, Richard, thank you.

After he unveiled the memorial bench, Richard invited us to say a few words of our own about Bill, and our time at Camp up to its fortieth year. Owen Lewis spoke about how he came to be invited to join Bill’s happy band of volunteers (which is actually documented in detail in my second book).

A quiz about the Camp’s history, prepared by Kim Harris, followed, before the raffle was drawn.

One of the highlights of the time we spent at Camp, I thought, was the visit of Annie’s two sons, Mark and Paul, with their wives, and children (all boys). Annie asked me to give a brief talk regarding her dad’s work on Camp, to better inform her lads about the enormous effort that their late grandfather had put in to get the Camp, his Camp, to what it became from its early roots. I felt honoured that she had asked me, but couldn't avoid a tear or two, because 1989/90 kept whispering to me as I spoke to Bill's grandsons and great grandsons.

We committed our thoughts of that very special weekend to the memorial book:

*29th June 2019*

*A memorable couple of days, filled with fun and laughter. Great company, who have become very good friends*

*Remembering Camp, and especially my lovely Dad - Bill Williams*

*Thanks Alan for making this happen*

*Ann Lewis*

*(Annie)*

*29th June 2019*

*A great weekend with good friends, to celebrate a man I was lucky to call my father; Bill Williams, who started the Longmynd Adventure Camp.*

*We are here to unveil a bench in memory of him.*

*A good day had by all.*

*Deb Williams (Bridge)*

*29th June 2019 1000hrs*

*Today we gather at Camp to honour its Founder, Chair and Skipper, the late Mr Bill Williams BEM.*

*We are unveiling a memorial bench to Bill. The unveiling 'ceremony' will be conducted by BISHOP RICHARD LEWIS, a former member of Bill's voluntary staff during the Camp's early years; and a valued family friend.*

*Thanks Richard. But above all, thanks to you Bill. God bless you Skipper; and thank you for everything you did for me and my brothers and many hundreds like us.*

*Alan Scriven MBE (Camp beneficiary; Camp staff 1965-1998)*

*28th June 2019*

*I arrived at Camp for a weekend with staff from past Camps; driving through the gates, memories soon came back. Happy memories, for I was 'home' with people I am proud to call very special friends, or even family.*

*Thank you Bill "Skipper" Williams for allowing me to be part of this amazing place which has got so many memories for children to carry into their adult lives. You will never be forgotten Skipper. Rest in Peace.*

*Kevin Duggins (Camp staff 80s + 90s)*

*29th June 2019*

*Fond memories of a wonderful time*

*Chris Toolan (Camp staff 1960s/70s)*

*29$^{th}$ June 2019*

*I was one of the 60s boys. Good times; good memories, and great to meet up with some of the other boys again.*

*God bless*

*Charlie Gunter (Camp 1961)*

*29$^{th}$ June 2019*

*Amazing to be back at Camp with so many good friends*

*Like we had never been away*

*Lyn and Mia (Mansell girls)*

*29$^{th}$ June 2019*

*Great to be back after over 50 years!*

*Lenny and Edwin Badger*

*(Camp boys 1960s)*

*29$^{th}$ June 2019*

*Fabulous memories of an amazing man, and lovely to meet again old faces... and new faces of people who knew Bill*

*Big THANK YOU*

*Richard Lewis*

*29$^{th}$ June 2019*

*Amazing to be back at Camp with wonderful friends, and so many memories*

*Kim Harris (Shropshire WRVS Children's Holiday Officer)*

*29th June 2019*

*We are friends of Ann. Heard so much about Camp - nice to see it at last. Also, we were neighbours of Bill in Shrewsbury.*

*30th June 2019*

*Never forget Bill Williams! What a legend!!!*

*It's been a Ball: Thank you*

*Dean Nightingale (Camp beneficiary + Camp staff) 1980s/1990s*

*01 July 2019*

*The time has come for me to say farewell to amazing people. But God willing, we will return together to the Longmynd Adventure Camp to continue our memories of this blessed land.*

*Thanks again*

*Kevin (the "Bulldog") Duggins.*

*(Camp staff 1980s/90s)*

Thank you to everyone who took the time to write their own brief message in our memorial book. If anyone who is reading this who was there on the day, but forgot to write a message, don't worry; your contribution to that wonderful weekend speaks volumes.

Below is the last-ever letter to be penned by a beneficiary of the Longmynd Adventure Camp; the final one of hundreds written over the best part of five decades (mainly to Bill Williams, obviously) after a holiday at Camp. It was written to me by Leon Preston, a member of tent two on the first of the two Camps of 1997:

*Dear Skipper*

*I miss you. I enjoyed playing football with you. I have told my mum about you and the leaders, and my mum said she was happy to know I was being looked after while I was away.*

*I liked it there because it was nice to go to the mountain and do all the things I had done while I was there, going to Rhyl that is, and going to the swimming baths.*

*I kept going to the arcade while we were at Rhyl.*

*I just want to say thank you for looking after me when I was at Camp. Please tell Dean that I miss him as well, and everyone else.*

*I will close now and I hope you will write back, or phone me. My phone number is 01706 ******

*Love from Leon*

A better argument for continuing the Camps in the format it was created for (which I have constantly - without apology - banged on about over my three books), you would never achieve. This lad, bless him, came to Camp for the first and last time, and he loved it... as did the vast majority of lads who came over the years. It is nothing short of tragic that it was stopped so suddenly and, in my humble opinion, disgracefully.

During the 1990s, the committee produced a constitution of sorts; and at the same time, a "Camp Charter". Whilst bearing in mind the correspondence between Living Proof and the LAC representative during the autumn of 1996; and part of the demands of the WRVS Children's Holiday Officer, please consider some "interesting" excerpts of both documents below:

*The CONSTITUTION (LAC reg. Charity no. 508293):*

*Objective:* *(part of)*

*To provide country holidays to socially deprived and under privileged children, to enable them to gain a sense of social responsibility and improve their characters in a friendly but disciplined environment.*

*It shall be a long-term objective to enable such children as are deemed capable to return as future staff members.*

*Aims and Responsibilities:* *(part of)*

*The Long Mynd* Adventure Camp Committee shall administer the Camp site and its accompanying assets in such a way as to provide such holidays at the Camp staffed completely by volunteer staff...*

*The Committee shall be responsible to the Charities Commissioners for all matters appertaining to the operation of the Camp site.*

*All members of the committee are considered to be trustees of the Charity and shall abide by the rules of the Charity Commissioners.*

*<u>Amendments to the Constitution:</u>*

*The Constitution may be amended by a Resolution passed by a 2/3 majority of those present and voting at any Ordinary meeting of the committee provided that notice is given in writing stating the terms of the Resolution to be proposed thereat shall have been sent to all members of the Committee not less than fourteen days before the date of the meeting, also providing that no amendment of Clauses 2 & 3 (Objective and Aims and Responsibilities) shall be made without the approval of the Court of the Charity Commissioners or other authority having jurisdiction under the Charities Act 1992.*

*Note 'Longmynd' is written as two words: 'Long Mynd'....as in the Camp Charter (below).

-----------------------------------------------------------------

*<u>The CAMP CHARTER:</u>*

*REMEMBER - In all things <u>the child's welfare</u> is paramount.*

*<u>Statement of Purpose and Function: (part of)</u>*

*The Long Mynd Adventure Camp exists for the purpose of providing holidays in the South Shropshire Hills for socially deprived and underprivileged children, at a site between Minton and Hamperley.*

*The Camp is a basic outdoor facility where the children will sleep in groups, in either tents or 12 bunk dormitories, each under the supervision of a group leader...*

*Staffing: (part of)*

*All Staff will be asked to declare any criminal convictions appertaining to children in any form or connection whatsoever, and due regard should be given to any offences which might compromise the health, safety or welfare of the children.*

*As all staff are voluntary, there is no inference given that the staff are trained to a high level in Child Care or Social Work. All staff however shall be accepted by the Camp Leader as being appropriately competent...*

*Any specialised activities shall be under the guidance and care of qualified personnel.*

-------------------------------------------------------------

All I ask is that the reader, after considering everything appertaining to the sudden end to the LAC's annual Camping Holidays for socially deprived children, in the format it had worked to from 1959 to 1997, and the excerpts listed above, at least consider the possibility that I might have an "axe to grind" on behalf of the children who may have missed out...

# Epilogue

To say it has been a pleasure to take on the self-imposed task of writing the history of the first forty years of a registered charity which I was very much involved with for thirty-three years, and to offer my readers (to whom I am sincerely very grateful for so much support and encouragement) a glimpse or two into the life of a boy born into a very poor family, is a complete understatement! It has at times, however, been an emotional and very mixed "ride", when I consider that nothing has been omitted. The highs and lows have, I hope, contributed to making all three books a good and interesting read.

At times I wondered whether it was worth continuing; I had the memorabilia to work from (I kept everything over the years, and was gifted valuable material to assist me), and the memories from my life. But I just kept thinking that no one, outside of people actually connected to "the Camp", would be interested. I was pleasantly proved wrong!

My life today is very different from my childhood and teenage years spent at 127 Fifth Avenue, Wolverhampton. But I haven't changed; I'm still the generous, grumpy, anti-social bastard (literally) I have always been.

But I now have a family I can actually feel a part of: my sons

Marc and Tom; their loved ones, and my sons' mother, Tina.

Being awarded the MBE was an honour I didn't see coming. I never asked for it (as if you can), or expected it, and to be honest, it showed me who my true friends (and family) were: those who were happy for me.

I left school in 1968, with no qualifications whatsoever to my name, but it didn't stop me rising to the top positions (from the lowest) in the majority of companies I have worked for. Still, the biggest achievement of my life, I feel, was being chosen by Bill Williams, to work with him, side by side, running the Boys Camps from 1980, for ten glorious years. Yes, our friendship soured for a while, but we clawed it back... just in time, as it happened!

From the very first time I met Bill, I took to him completely, as did so many others. He was a one-off; very special. He was a truly remarkable man I felt honoured to know as a very valued friend. It's a travesty beyond words that formal recognition for Bill's outstanding contribution to society, be it through his police career or his stand-out work for all the charities etc of which he was a member, amounted only (with no disrespect intended) to the British Empire Medal by the Lord Lieutenant of Shropshire in 1983. If ever a man deserved a knighthood, it is Mr William Frederick Williams!

They can be awarded posthumously... can't they?

It is a pity and a shame that things turned out the way they did in the late nineties. I have no way of knowing or proving that dispensing with our traditional format of Camp operations was with the full knowledge of the committee (with the exception of myself, obviously) in order to turn the premises into what it became post-1998. But if there's one word of truth in it, and it does at least smack of something not being right (when everything is considered), then the person(s) responsible should hang their head(s) in shame!

It still angers me to read the occasional splurge written (or spoken) by some "Johnny-come-lately" current committee member, or "friend of the Camp", about how it began, and what is has become, because evidently what they actually know about the real history of the place could be carved on the back of an aspirin!

Our group Minton Memories is focused now on realising our latest intention, to further honour Mr W.F. Williams BEM with a head and shoulders "bust", to be positioned in a location agreeable to his daughters Annie and Debbie. We will also strive to have a Blue Plaque made in honour of his outstanding and selfless charity work.

God bless you, Skipper, and thank you again; from all of us who had the honour of touching your life, as you touched all of ours in the most beautiful and memorable of ways.

Love, Light and Peace, Sir.

# Longmynd Adventure Camp Roll

# Call of Senior Staff:

**Bill Williams BEM:** Founder of the LAC. Committee Chair; Skipper 1958 – 1989inc'; 1997 (part-time).

**Alan Scriven MBE:** 'Skipper' 1979; 1990 -1995inc', and 1997 (part time) 'Bosun' 1980 -1989 incl.

**David Scriven:** 'Bosun' 1990.

**Alan Preece:** 'Skipper' 1996. 'Bosun' 1991- 1993 incl.; 1995

**Stephan Latewood:** 'Bosun' 1994.

**Marc Scriven:** 'Bosun' 1996; 1997.

---

To close this third and final book on the Camp, I would like to offer my thanks in no particular order (on behalf of the many other "kindred spirits") to some other kind souls who responded to a calling; a calling to what was undoubtedly a small but grandly beautiful piece of heaven on earth, for your part in making it so...

And to those who may have slipped under my radar (of records), my sincere apologies accompany my heartfelt thanks.

John Price
Richard Edwards
Jeremy Eyre
Henry Edwards
Harry Cartwright
Duncan Richards
Tony Foster
Bob Moore
John Hallet
Bill Berry
Cadet Hemmings
Peter Taylor
David Hall
Roy Holdsworth
John Hollick
Eddie James
Ian "Scottie" Gibbons

Paul Wood
David Drew
Gordon Swan
John Walker
Cadet
Dave Willetts
Mick Payne
Chris Nicholls
Eric Bullion
Stuart McConkey
Bob Weaver
Trevor Purcell
Neil Broom
Wayne Lloyd
Peter Shaw
Melvyn Beard
Rob Sheldon

Peter Mead
Steve Dixon
Barry Carl
Bob Nickles
Glyn Evans
John Rowland
Michael Peacock
Neil Williams
Mike Holloran
John Scott Jones
Michael Knight
Tim Tonks

Owen J. Lewis (for his kind contributions to all my books)

Catherine Clarke (for the cover design on this and my previous books).

And finally, to Katharine Smith (Heddon Publishing), who has patiently supported and encouraged my dream to write the history (in a trilogy of books) of a much-loved children's charity; and also episodes of my life within it.

www.ingramcontent.com/pod-product-compliance
Ingram Content Group UK Ltd.
Pitfield, Milton Keynes, MK11 3LW, UK
UKHW041431210726
13854UKWH00010B/1854

9 781913 166441